Contents

The Deadly Story Starts Here!

The mission was simplicity itself: track down 60 deadly animals from all over the world, and find out (and capture on film) just what makes them deadly. It sounds easy enough for a team of experienced wildlife film-makers, but it was a challenge that took me and the Deadly 60 team to every corner of the world, testing us to the limits, and often putting our lives in genuine danger.

My job as a naturalist has taken me around the world countless times and shown me bizarre and beautiful creatures far stranger than any you'll find in myths and legends. Wherever I've gone, I've found that a fascination for certain kinds of animal is shared by everyone I've met, from the Sea Gypsies of the South China Sea to holy Babas in Bengal and the Korowai cannibals of New Guinea. While we may be charmed by the cute and furry creatures of the world we reserve our greatest fascination for the most fearsome animals, whether large or small – those with devastating predatory powers and dazzling defensive abilities. Shaolin monks studied the movements of the tiny praying mantis to develop their martial arts; Hindu holymen have entire temples devoted to the hypnotic wonder of the cobra; the ancient Maya worshipped jaguars, scorpions and eagles; and the Australian Aborigines devote Dreamtime legends to snakes and spiders.

It makes total sense to me; as a kid, I was nothing like as interested in koalas and baby chimps, but I could rattle off endless stats and facts about tigers, eagles and sharks. The year-long Deadly 60 mission gave me the chance to make all the fantasies of my childhood come true, and have adventures beyond even my wildest dreams!

Right from the early days of Deadly 60, I was determined to make a series that really told the truth about the wild animals people think are dangerous. I wanted people to share my fascination with some of nature's finest predators but not to be afraid; after all, wild animals around the world very rarely actually hurt anyone. The world's most venomous snake has never killed a human being, and experts say that you're more likely to be killed by a falling vending machine than by a shark. To be honest, I'm sick and tired of films, TV programmes and books trying to convince us that snakes and sharks are desperate to tear us all to shreds – it's just not true. I've dived with every reputedly dangerous species of shark and caught every lethal species of snake (let's face it, I'm asking for trouble!) and I'm still here.

I thought it would be much more interesting to look at what makes animals deadly to other animals. Why does a cuttlefish create its dazzling light display?

Which animal has the fastest strike in the animal kingdom? Why are the African Wild Dogs the most efficient predators on the African plains? Why do some snakes have venom that could kill an elephant when they feed on tiny mice?

Deadly 60 is just a selection of the world's dangerous animals. There are so many to choose from that we couldn't ever hope to fit them all in, and I apologize in advance if your favourite is not included. We weren't able to film absolutely everything we'd have liked to, and to make matters worse, I had a really bad rock-climbing fall in the middle of the the year. I broke my back and smashed up my foot, which really put a spanner in the works! Orca, Giant Squid, Komodo Dragons and Leopard Seals are just a few we missed, which convinces me we could easily do another 60...

Watch this space!

However, we had plenty of time just to wander about in the bush looking for stuff, and we came up with some wonderful surprises we could never have planned for.

Deadly 60 is not just about the animals. Our crew is a tight-knit family of wildlife-crazy film-makers, who followed me around the world for months on end. Big boss John Miller joined us after working with survival guru (and one of my heroes) Ray Mears. Burly director James Brickell is a biologist and film-maker who's directed everyone from Simon King to the great legend David Attenborough, and came to us fresh from producing *Life In Cold Blood*, the iconic series on reptiles and amphibians. Like me, James has a passion for reptiles, and it took the influence of everyone else on the series to prevent us making every single mission about finding snakes! Second director Rosie Gloyns had put aside a career as a primatologist (a monkey scientist) working in the jungles of Gabon in order to work with us. She's a real role model for any hard-as-nails girls out there who'd love a life chasing wildlife, and was inevitably the only person I could convince to allow me to hang off ropes over impossible chasms and paddle through death-dealing high seas... mostly because she was secretly desperate to do it all herself!

Our two camera crews rotated every month or so. The first soundman was former artillery soldier Rich Whitley, an extremely funny character and resident tough guy. Mark Vinall was on camera. Mark has been my cameraman for the last eight years, and we've been through hell and high water together. Over the years he's developed almost a sixth sense for what crazy thing I'm about to do next, and in all that time he's never missed a single important shot. A Humpback Whale leaps from the water without

warning alongside our boat; a baby gorilla silently wanders out of the jungle and takes me by the hand, a rare frog boings from a bush into my face, and I turn around and Mark has miraculously captured the whole thing.

The other camera unit was made up of soundman Nick Allinson – jungle expert, mad keen fisherman and former professional shark-feeder – and Belfast-born cameraman Jonny Rogers. Jonny and I have been through some hardcore expeditions together, including abseiling into a vast unknown jungle sinkhole and dropping into the pit of hell at the bottom of one of the world's highest waterfalls. He's a tough little fella with endless humour when things get bad; a great person to have on any team.

Underwater camerawork was handled by Mark and also by Simon Enderby, a marine biologist and one of the world's finest sub-marinal film-makers. There are few better people to be in the water with when you're dodging Tiger Sharks!

While these teams were on the front line, the people working away in the office, charming far-off customs officials and editing the footage we brought home into meaningful programmes, and the bigwigs who made sure we had enough money and looked in horror at our risk assessments (the forms which spell out all the dangerous things you'll be doing) all played a massive role in making it happen.

As for which animal is top of the list, well, it's a question I'm often asked, and could talk about for hours and hours. Truth is, there is no easy answer. How can you compare the skills of a shark and a snake when they feed on different things in different environments? Is the mosquito the deadliest animal of all because of the disease-causing parasites it hosts and spreads, or should the parasites be considered the killers? No easy answers but a whole lot of interesting questions; and if that gets you asking about nature, I'll be a happy man!

Opposite page, left to right James Brickell, John Miller, Rosie Gloyns.
This page, clockwise from top left Rich Whitley, Nick Allinson, Jonny Rogers, Simon Enderby, Mark Vinall.

Hippopotamus

Hippopotamus amphibius

With a big male weighing in at up to 3.5 tonnes – as much as a pick-up truck – armed with ivory tusks that can be as long as swords and an attitude that is best described as ferociously unpredictable, the Hippopotamus is Africa's most dangerous large animal, killing more people than lions or even crocs.

Those huge tusks are overgrown teeth; no good for feeding, but ideal for maiming other hippos – and people. However, hippos are vegetarians with placid natures – unless you get in their way. When they think their territory or calves are being threatened, hippos can flip their lids in the blink of an eye. My first experience of this was as a young boy out on a Kenyan lake in a wooden rowboat. We must have inadvertently come between a mother hippo and her calf and she launched towards us, creating a bow wave like a battleship. Our local guide leapt to the front of the boat and beat her off with his paddle while we cowered behind him!

Calm before the storm

Twenty-five years later, I went to a suitable African river, me in a kayak, and Mark the camera-man in an inflatable boat, to get close to hippos in the wild. Our first hippo was floating languidly in a dark green pool with fast-flowing water running through it. We spent most of the day watching him. Whenever we got close, he'd just duck underwater and disappear for half an hour. He was about as frightening as pocket fluff.

We were all feeling a bit deflated. I did my last piece to camera, turned the kayak around, and then stopped dead. There was another hippo right in front of us. He had come downstream, and found us blocking the way to his feeding grounds.

We weren't all that concerned, but then he dropped silently beneath the water. He was out of my view, but his vast bulk was still visible to the rest of the crew who'd taken up position on the bank. James started commentating: 'OK, Steve, he's just in front of you, maybe 30 metres or so… Er, OK, so he's starting to head your way now… ooh, he's moving quite fast, 20 metres… hang on, 10 metres… 5… GO GO GO he's right there!'

Near miss

Absolute total panic. The people on land were screaming, the camera boat guys were towing their boat out of the water as the hippo came within metres of them, and I paddled off as fast as I could. It was terrifying, we couldn't see anything, but the guys on the side were yelling like we were about to get attacked (and having watched the footage back, it looks like we nearly were).

I paddled full steam up to the bank. James grabbed the front of my boat, and I honestly believe he could have dragged me – still in the boat – all the way to Cape Town and onto a plane home. Despite his ten

years in the Natural History Unit, producing gripping programmes like *Big Cat Diary*, he said candidly that it was the scariest moment of his career.

So the Hippopotamus makes the Deadly 60 for its power, attitude, aggression and most of all unpredictability. There's no rulebook for how a hippo will behave.

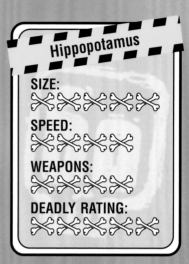

Hippopotamus

SIZE:
☠ ☠ ☠ ☠ ☠

SPEED:
☠ ☠ ☠ ☠

WEAPONS:
☠ ☠ ☠

DEADLY RATING:
☠ ☠ ☠ ☠ ☠

Left Hippos will give a massive yawn like this if you get too close for comfort. They're not tired, they're taking an opportunity to show off those remarkable tusks and let you know who's boss!

Black Mamba
Dendroaspis polylepis

Ask any African person what their deadliest snake is, and you'll get the same answer every time – the Black Mamba is the one everybody fears the most. The second longest venomous snake in the world, it grows up to 4.5 metres long. That's more than two of me lying head to toe!

A Black Mamba's bite yields an enormous amount of venom; some experts say there's enough of it in each mouthful to kill 40 people.

You don't want to be one of those 40 – it would be a horrible, painful way to go, with your lungs and heart shutting down, bleeding from your eyes, nose, and ears, and your nervous system in total agonizing freeflow.

However, just like so many other dangerous animals around the world, the fact that every mamba's bite could *potentially* kill people doesn't mean that mambas actually *do* very much people-killing.

Donald Strydom, my African snake-catching hero, guru and pal, is fond of pointing out that in Africa death by snakebite is rare.

He even says it's so rare that you're actually more likely to die from an infected bite from another person than from a snake's bite!

Mamba myths

There is more nonsense written about Black Mambas than just about any other snake on the planet. People say they can scoot along the ground faster than a racehorse can run, and that they will chase human beings for hundreds of metres trying to attack and bite them.

Well, I tested this out with a mamba in the African bush, running after it with my video camera. Far from chasing me, it just did everything it could to

get away from me and escape into the nearest bush. If anything the mamba is more comfy up in the trees than on the ground, and as it slithered off at full speed, I could easily keep pace with it at a gentle jog. Even so, it holds the record for the world's fastest snake, with a top speed of about six miles per hour.

Warning signs

When a Black Mamba coils its body into an S-shape ready to launch its lightning-speed strike, and it reveals the impressive fangs and jet-black interior of its mouth, you'll know you are looking at one of the world's most perfectly formed snakes. You'll also know it's time to back off, fast.

Though it's not the aggressive maniac that its bad press makes out, a cornered mamba will do what it has to do to deal with a threat, and we are lucky that its character is not as venomous as the contents of its fangs.

Its speed, agility, climbing skills and that deadly bite are all hunting weapons, and while it's not a threat to us unless we threaten it first, a Black Mamba is still a formidable predator. The small mammals and birds it feeds on really don't stand a chance.

So that's why the Black Mamba is on my Deadly 60, not because it's a danger to us, but because it's

one of the great natural wonders of the world, a sizzling, speedy strategist of a serpent.

Black Mamba

SIZE:
✕✕✕✕✕

SPEED:
✕✕✕✕✕

WEAPONS:
✕✕✕✕✕

DEADLY RATING:
✕✕✕✕✕

Below It's not surprising there is so much myth surrounding the mystical mamba. Some of its reputation is well earned. Able to deal death in single bite, it's one of the finest serpent stars on the list.

Transvaal Fat-tailed Scorpion

Parabuthus transvaalicus

There are some 2,000 different species of scorpion worldwide, but only about 25 are potentially dangerous. I've lost count of the stings I've had, and only one cost me a night's sleep – the others were like wasp stings. However, if I were to get on the wrong end of this wee beastie, it would be a very different story.

Scorpions. They had huge claws and spindly tails, and their stings were almost painless.

The anatomy of the Fat-tailed Scorpion is the other way around – the claws are much thinner, but the tail is broad as my finger.

Critter catching

I had confidently told everyone that as we were in South Africa in the summer, slogging through 45°C heat every day, we would not need tents and could just sleep out under the stars. Later I lay down beside the fire, feeling sheepish as lightning crackled across the sky and spots of rain fizzed in the ashes.

Luckily, the clouds gave way to a dazzling starry sky, where every constellation stood out like join-the-dots, and every

The Transvaal Fat-tailed Scorpion has venom more potent than the Diamondback Rattlesnake of America, and it can even flick this lethal fluid from the end of its tail towards the eyes of an attacker. Its venom works in a similar way to the Black Mamba's and receiving a dose of it could be equally serious. That's pretty impressive for an animal that would fit into a cigarette packet.

Searching in the bushveld of South Africa, most of the scorpions we'd been finding under the rocks were Flat Rock star competed for our attention with the distant calls from beasts of the bush.

Donald – my South African snake-catching hero – told us long stories about lions and hyenas staking out people who'd been daft enough to sleep out like this and towing them off to their deaths.

In my night wanders, I first caught a small and very angry Puff Adder which I nearly added to the list, but then at last I found a Fat-tailed Scorpion by searching with my ultraviolet torch. Scorpions glow bright yellow under UV light – probably so they can see other scorpions hiding in crevices and can give them a wide berth.

I saw the bright yellow shape disappearing into a bush and leaped after it, taking the high-risk strategy of catching it by putting my fingers on either side of the stinger. Don't ever try that yourself – get it wrong and you will get stung!

Like all scorpions, Fat-tails use their claws and sting to kill small insects. The scorpions are in turn prey for larger animals – those that are brave enough.

Blown away

I was about to pay the price for catching this one, though not in the way you might expect.

Just seconds after I'd caught it, and was holding it by the tail with the UV torch in my other hand, there was an explosion that made us all jump about a foot in the air.

We realised later that the batteries inside my UV torch had blown up!

As one of the most potently venomous scorpions in the world, and one that can flick its toxins as accurately as a spitting cobra, the Transvaal Fat-tailed Scorpion is a definite for the list. Miraculously, I managed to avoid throwing the deadliest invertebrate in Africa straight into the cameraman's lap!

Fat-tailed Scorpion

SIZE:
SPEED:
WEAPONS:
DEADLY RATING:

Left Able to flick venom from the end of its tail, and one of the few species of scorpion in the world that is potentially dangerous to humans, the Transvaal Fat-tailed Scorpion is a wonder among invertebrates.

Nile Crocodile

Crocodylus niloticus

The Nile Crocodile vies with the Saltwater Crocodile of Australasia for the title of world's largest reptile. Reports vary wildly about how big they actually get; seven metres is a good bet, though there are reports of over nine metres.

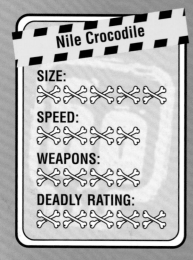

Nile Crocodile

SIZE:

SPEED:

WEAPONS

DEADLY RATING:

For every few centimetres longer a croc gets, it gets much bigger, broader and heavier. Therefore a five-metre croc dwarfs one of four metres, and even a four-metre croc needs to spend most of its day in the water, as it is too heavy to support its vast bulk on land.

The gargantuan beasts you see pulling wildebeest into the waters on TV wildlife programmes are probably no bigger than 5 metres long.

Why be any larger, when you can bite down on your prey or enemies with three tonnes of force?

Jaws for thought

The Nile Crocodile is all about stealth and short bursts of blinding speed. As a cold-blooded animal, it gains most of its energy from the sun and does not need to eat every day or even every month.

Some studies show that crocs may only need the energy equivalent of a Mars Bar a day! Because they don't have to be constantly on the hunt for food, they can wait motionless, submerged with just eyes and nostrils above the water, until exactly the right moment arrives to attack. The prey is mostly fish, but crocs will also eat large mammals.

The jaw hinges like a trapdoor and cannot move side to side, so a croc can't chew. Instead, it clamps its mouth closed on its prey, then spins its entire body (which can weigh as much as a car) in a manic death roll. Huge chunks of flesh are torn out of the unlucky prey and swallowed whole.

Brush-off

The Deadly 60 Nile Croc experience was a bit of a let-down. We went to a game reserve to see a 2.5-metre female who had been making regular appearances at a waterhole.

When we turned up, she was lying in the shade in a perfect position for filming. Having worked with crocodiles over the years, I have a good sense of how close you can safely get to them when they're out of the water; most won't chase you for more than a few metres and are more likely to retreat than attack.

However, just as I had turned to camera to start talking, our guide lunged behind me with a long-poled swimming pool brush, and started prodding her with it. Every time she so much as twitched he'd scream 'Quick, run!'. Then he'd poke her with the brush and dash for the bushes. The annoyed croc soon shuffled out of sight!

The next plan was to tempt her out with a bit of meat. It was perfect; she moved into position just as I started talking to camera. Then the guide threw her another chunk of meat, which she scoffed as if at a performing croc show. The guide (brush in hand) paused briefly behind me to look into the camera and James put his hands over his face in despair.

But even though you can sometimes fight one off with an oversized broom, if you fell into a river where a Nile Crocodile was waiting for lunch, you wouldn't stand a chance. They are near perfect death-dealing dragons, and definitely on the Deadly 60!

Below One of the very few creatures I would NOT get in the water with, the Nile Crocodile is truly master of its environment.

African Hunting Dog

Lycaon pictus

Though a natural contender for the Deadly 60, African Hunting Dogs are also very rare and hard to see. I personally hadn't seen them in the wild for 20 years, and we were all pretty certain that the two days we'd set apart to find them would not be anything like enough. However, there is so much that's outstanding about their behaviour and abilities that we just had to try.

Above They may look like slightly mangy mongrels, but these dogs are truly among the finest and most successful predators in Africa. Living proof that cooperation works!

African Hunting Dogs work in packs of up to 60, pursuing their prey (animals up to the size of Cape Buffalo and Eland) at speeds of up to 45 miles per hour. Unlike big cats, which specialize in short bursts of speed and give up if they don't get immediate success, these dogs are relentless, and will chase prey until it is totally exhausted.

This incredible endurance makes them probably the most efficient predators in Africa – around 80% of hunts result in a kill. Some groups of lions only make a kill in 10% of hunts.

To give us the best chance of finding the dogs, I took a long flight in a microlight over the southern Kruger National Park in South Africa, hoping to catch sight of them. It was a marvellous flight, and I got awesome views of elephants, rhinos and huge herds of giraffes, but no dogs.

Dog gone

The next stage in the plan was to show just how hard it was for the dogs to stalk their prey, so I dressed up in camouflage and tried to stalk some game. This was a lot tougher than you might think, as the weather had been so dry that moving through the vegetation was louder than walking on cornflakes. However, after a while I did manage to get pretty close to some wildebeest and a giraffe – enough to make the point I guess, though I did look a bit daft.

The next day I upped the stakes. We were staying in a house right in the bush with no fences or protection of any kind, and the next morning while having breakfast, someone pointed out a very large male elephant. Although he was the size of a caravan, he would just wander behind a bush and totally disappear, so filming him was a nightmare. Eventually he headed to a nearby waterhole, so we decided to follow him.

Hunting high and low

Here, the camera crew could use a viewing platform above the water and be totally safe, and I could sneak in closer to him on the ground. As I edged forward, I weighed up how fast he'd be able to get to where I was, and how quickly I could reach the viewing platform. He helpfully moved around the watering hole so that the water was between us, which I figured would slow him down if he did charge. In the end I was no more than 10 metres away from a totally wild elephant. I was splashed with droplets of water as he sprayed trunkfuls of water and mud all over himself, and could see every wrinkle, every hair, every scar on his hide.

We didn't find the dogs but that's no reason why the wonderful African Hunting Dog shouldn't make it on to the Deadly 60. Giving new meaning to the term 'dogged determination', the wild dog is on the list for its phenomenal team work and its unprecedented kill rate.

Right Those big ears are full of blood vessels which allow the dog to cool down after long chases.

African Hunting Dog

SIZE:
✕✕✕

SPEED:
✕✕✕

WEAPONS:
✕✕✕✕

DEADLY RATING:
✕✕✕✕✕

African Fish Eagle

Haliaeetus vocifer

Throughout our time in southern Africa, we'd seen African Fish Eagles circling over the cliffs around us, and managed to get some footage of them in the wild, but the real star was a (fairly) tame eagle called Bono – so named because of his distinctive singing voice.

African Fish Eagle

SIZE:
✕✕✕✕✕

SPEED:
✕✕✕✕✕

WEAPONS:
✕✕✕✕✕

DEADLY RATING:
✕✕✕✕✕

Bono had been taken from the wild as a chick illegally, and eventually rescued for a bird centre by comedy falconry double act Mark and Mark, two English guys who are about as serious as the Chuckle Brothers.

Bono was just magnificent. With his black body and white head he looked much like a Bald Eagle, but bigger – so big and heavy that after just a few minutes holding him, I felt like my arm was about to drop off

His talons were as sharp as fishing hooks, and when he looked into my eyes with his hooked beak just inches from my face, I have to admit to having a little worried tingle in my tummy.

Eagle school

The real highlight of the filming sequence was Bono showing us how fish eagles hunt. This was far from easy because Bono has never been a truly wild eagle, and had never caught fish for himself. Mark and Mark first had to wean him off his diet of chicken and beef, and get him down to fighting weight, as well as trying to rouse his natural instinct to hunt.

When they first started his lessons, using a handy rubber training fish, Bono tried to catch it not with his talons as he should, but with his beak. This resulted in him crash-landing in the water, somersaulting head-over-heels, and nearly drowning.

When he finally got to shore, he decided to take his anger and humiliation out on the closest person, so one of the Marks had a vicious bird of prey basically trying to rip him to shreds. After more attempts he finally mastered it, and we hoped he'd perform on cue for us.

We took Bono to a wild lake surrounded by mountains. His screaming soon attracted several wild fish eagles which hung around in the trees nearby to watch.

Mark II threw the rubber fish in front of me. Bono made his first pass, but pulled up at the last minute. Ten minutes later he whooshed past again, but didn't go anywhere near the fish, and flew straight up to the top of a tree. The third time was perfect. He scorched down out of the tree, skimmed the surface of the water, lifted at the last minute, snatched the fish from the water, then flew straight into a bush.

Fishing tackle

When Mark finally extricated him and rescued the plastic trout we decided to try again.

Pass four was another refusal. As I went down to retrieve the fish,

I heard a noise behind me — Bono had taken off unbidden, and was swooping straight at my head! I dropped to the ground as his wingtips brushed my ears, and he effortlessly plucked the fish from in front of me. In the wild, this behaviour is so effective that these eagles only need to fish for 10 minutes a day.

So when people talk about 'eagle eyes' they are right on the money. The African Fish Eagle is lightning-fast, tooled up with tearing talons, and the first bird on the Deadly 60.

Below Up close you can really appreciate the great power of this ruthless hunter.

Great White Shark

Carcharodon carcharias

I guess a lot of people would agree that the most obvious animal on our list has to be that huge biting machine, the Great White Shark. The largest Great White ever captured was 6.4 metres long and 4.5 metres around – it weighed nearly 3.5 tonnes, and several lorries were needed to tow it away!

Great White Shark

SIZE:
✕✕✕✕✕✕

SPEED:
✕✕✕✕✕✕

WEAPONS:
✕✕✕✕✕✕

DEADLY RATING:
✕✕✕✕✕✕

The measured bite of a three-metre shark pushes four tonnes of pressure through every square centimetre of tooth. Those huge, razor-sharp teeth can kill a big seal with a single, decisive strike.

However, shark attacks worldwide are absolutely insignificant as a cause of human death. Four or five a year is pretty average, and there was just one death for the whole of 2007! Though people seem to love the image of the man-eating Great White inspired by the film *Jaws*, these magnificent creatures actually live most of their lives as far away from people as possible and little is known about their lifecycle.

Great white waves

I'd filmed Great Whites before from a cage, but my life's ambition was to freedive with them outside of a cage. We'd found a dive operation in South Africa who were willing to make it happen for us, and so with mounting excitement we made our way down the coast. Things had been going well for the guys there in the weeks leading up to our visit; they'd dived with the sharks on several occasions, and got some amazing photos. However, we woke up the next morning to see huge white waves out at sea and bad weather made our mission impossible for three days. Things were no better on our last day.

We had no choice but to head out to sea and at least try and find something. So, with dread in our stomachs, we drove our inflatable boat out through hectic seas (all getting drenched in the process), and dropped some bait into the water. While we waited, Mark the cameraman provided amusement with some creative vomiting – he would suddenly hand the camera to someone next to him, calmly announce, 'I'm going to vomit now,' then turn and projectile hurl, with a noise like a seal being shredded by a Great White. In keeping with the warts and all feeling of the series, James began filming Mark as he yodelled noisily over the side, before panning back to me to comment on his performance.

Feeding frenzy

Then, halfway through chuckling to camera, I blurted excitedly: 'GREAT WHITE SHARK!' About 60 metres off the side of the boat, scything through the waves at a terrific pace, was the familiar and chilling dark shape of the famous fin, with the silhouette beneath of a three-metre shark. As we scrabbled all over each other and our dive cylinders, the shark effortlessly cut the water apart and was on the bait. She threshed around the buoys, dragging them beneath the surface, ripping at the fish heads with her brutal teeth. It was absolute chaos.

The first shark soon left, but a second one played for much longer. I took the underwater housing, and tried to get shots of the animal as she dove beneath the boat, centimetres away from my fingers. The third to turn up was big – over four metres – and more laid-back. She circled almost lazily around the bait, occasionally raising her head above the water to chomp down on the fish. By the time we headed for home, there had been four biggies and a tiny Hammerhead Shark the size of my leg, risking its life surfing around the big girls.

So I didn't get my dream encounter in the water, but I got close enough, and I don't think anyone's going to dispute the awesome Great White Shark's place on our list.

Below Many would argue that the Great White Shark should be at the top of the Deadly 60 list. There's no doubting who's the master when you're in their environment. If one of these wanted you for dinner, you wouldn't stand a chance.

Honey Badger

Mellivora capensis

I'm sure it will surprise some people to have a furry little animal included here – particularly one with such a soppy-sounding name, but the *Guinness Book of World Records* lists it as the 'most fearless animal on the planet'. It's a reputation the Honey Badger utterly deserves.

Honey Badgers may also be involved in a fascinating cooperative relationship with birds. Honeyguides are small African birds which like eating bee larvae and beeswax, but have no way of getting into a bee's nest. They guide native people to bee's nests with a special call. The bushmen then take the honey from the hive, leaving its remains for the birds. Some biologists think that honeyguides and Honey Badgers work together in a similar way, but no one has yet recorded the behaviour.

A Honey Badger is about as long as a man's arm, with a dark brown underside, and what looks like a dirty yellow cloak over its back. It has beady little eyes and a blunt snout. Cute though it is, the Honey Badger makes a Tasmanian Devil seem like a bunny rabbit. These animals are scared of absolutely nothing. They will devour everything from scorpions and cobras to three-metre pythons and even small crocodiles, and are even known to drive lions off their prey!

Buster's moves

In order to show quite how ferocious Honey Badgers can be, we'd arranged to hook up with Buster, a captive Honey Badger in a small animal sanctuary in the backwoods of South Africa. As soon as I stepped into her enclosure, Buster pounced. She ripped the padlock off the door – through the fence – and hauled it back through the wire with enormous but nimble claws. James and Rosie tried to stop her, and she turned into a snarling nightmare, sending them scuttling off squealing!

Once she had the padlock, Buster clutched it to her chest in one paw, and gambolled off to the burrow she'd dug in her run, adding her prize to the many other padlocks and flip-flops she had stashed there over the years.

In order to show Buster's true abilities, we took her out to forage in the wild for a few hours. As soon as she was put down on the ground, she was off, beetling away with her nose to the ground. I sprinted after her with a little camera, trying to give an impression of what it must be like to be a Honey Badger.

Although she was engrossed in her bumbling about, if I got a little too close she'd spin about with alarming ferocity. She was snapping her vicious jaws and uttering a guttural snarl so unsettling that even now, when I watch the footage back it makes me jump!

Sweet as honey?

Towards the end of filming, Buster was rewarded with a big plate of honey. She started to tuck in – an opportunity for me to sit behind her and do a piece to camera. All that was spoiling the shot was the plastic plate, so I decided to take it from her. Big mistake. At first, she'd just snarl out the corner of her mouth like a dog when you get too close to its food bowl. Then I actually touched the plate and she turned into a roaring, whirling dervish! When Rich tried to use the end of his sound pole to push the honey off the plate, she went utterly mental, screaming and gnashing, and threatening to turn the carbonfibre pole into expensive matchsticks.

Honey Badgers may not be big, but they're bad, and they're on the Deadly 60.

Honey Badger

SIZE:
☒☒☒

SPEED:
☒☒☒

WEAPONS:
☒☒☒☒☒

DEADLY RATING:
☒☒☒☒

Left Buster the badger, just before she went wild!
Below A Honey Badger takes on a Cape Cobra. Just after this photo was taken, the badger enjoyed a meal of one of Africa's most lethal snakes.

Blue-ringed Octopus

Hapalochlaena spp.

Quite possibly the most lethal venom of any animal we encountered filming the Deadly 60 comes from an unlikely looking little invertebrate, the Blue-ringed Octopus. I'd done quite a lot of research into these beasties whilst writing a book about venom, and everything I learned about them made me desperate to find one.

They're surprisingly tiny, with a head that's only rarely as large as a squash ball, and they are generally a dull yellowy-brown colour. But when they're excited they suddenly reveal neon blue rings all over their body and tentacles in one of the most stunning colour displays imaginable. This is a warning to take notice of, as the Blue-ring has a painless but lethal venom that can kill a person in just a few hours. One Australian woman found a Blue-ring and posed for a photo with it in her cleavage. She never felt the bite, but she died before the day was over.

Bottling it

Blue-rings are most active at night, and they like to hide in tiny holes, which makes them extremely difficult to find. Our first plan was to go out on a boat into a Western Australian harbour to look for rubbish. Literally. The octopuses often hole up inside old beer bottles or fizzy-drink cans that have been thrown into the sea by lazy fishermen, so our plan was to go looking for those. Unfortunately, I smashed down on the first bottle I found with the butt of my dive knife, driving straight through the glass and slicing the heel of my hand on the jagged edge. Blood began turning the water black-green, and as these waters are a stronghold of Great White Sharks I came straight back up to bandage my messy paw. It took three days of searching before we got lucky. Cameraman Mark and I were on a night dive underneath

Below It's one of the most toxic creatures on the list, but the bite is almost painless. You wouldn't know you were in trouble until way too late...

Bussleton jetty, a huge pier with an extraordinary array of life growing and living beneath it. I shone my torch into a crack in an old piece of timber on the sea bottom, and there it was, my first ever Blue-ring!

The net closes
Moving as if tip-toeing underwater, I set Mark up on the other side of the huge piece of wood, and placed the underwater lights just right to illuminate the scene. I had a small net in my pocket, and took the long wire handle and ever so gently eased it into the crack alongside the octopus. My plan was to quickly lever him out so we could see him before he got wind of my plan. I took a deep breath, shut off my air supply so as not to freak him out with my bubbles, and levered the net. It stuck. It caught fast on a barnacle and wouldn't move!

I worked away frantically trying to free the net and get the octopus out, but he had disappeared off into the timber.

We tried until our air ran out, but with no luck.

So we didn't get one on camera, but the Blue-ringed Octopus has to be a contender for the list. It's small enough to fit in your pocket, glows like a mini mobile disco, and has some of the most potent poison found on the planet.

Blue-ringed Octopus

SIZE:
✕

SPEED:
✕

WEAPONS:
✕ ✕ ✕ ✕ ✕

DEADLY RATING:
✕ ✕ ✕

Bottlenose Dolphin

Tursiops truncatus

Of all the animals on the Deadly 60, the Bottlenose Dolphin was the one that raised the most eyebrows – after all, they're everyone's favourite smiley-faced flipper flapper. However, when you remember this series is all about animals doing battle with other animals, the dolphin actually has a good shot at being top of the list.

Bottlenose Dolphin

SIZE:
🦴🦴🦴🦴

SPEED:
🦴🦴🦴🦴🦴

WEAPONS:
🦴🦴🦴🦴🦴🦴

DEADLY RATING:
🦴🦴🦴🦴🦴🦴

Why? Well, it's all about brains. Dolphins have a big brain (even larger and heavier than a human brain) which means they can 'talk' to each other in a complex way. The clicks, blips, chirps and whistles they use when interacting form a complete language, which allows them to coordinate their actions and hunt effectively in packs. They herd fish like dogs do with sheep, singling out weak individuals, and the actions of the team result in a better haul for all! Dolphins have even been known to herd fish onto dry land, purposefully beaching themselves in order to strand the fish.

Clickety click

Those clicks aren't just for talking to other dolphins, though – they are also weapons and tools in their own right. The way the echo sounds when it bounces back tells the dolphin everything it needs to know about what's in front of it – how far away it is, whether it's moving and in what direction, and whether it's a living thing or not. Dolphins keep up a constant barrage of clicks as they travel along, and by listening to the echoes of those clicks they build up a 'sound map' of everything around them. They can even use these echolocation skills to find sea creatures like octopuses hiding in the sands of the sea bottom, and they are said to use very loud clicks to actually stun fish in the water. From a fish's point of view, the dolphin is the most intelligent, super-evolved killing machine on the planet.

I have had loads of close encounters with Bottlenose Dolphins over the years, but my Deadly 60 outing was the best so far. We were armed with James Bond-esque scuba sleds – motorized underwater skidoos that pulled us along at near dolphin pace. As we didn't have to put any effort into swimming, we could freedive for several minutes at a time, dodging and weaving in a manner that the dolphins really seemed to enjoy copying.

Game on

All day long we had dolphins close to us, soaring alongside us, showing off that they could swim faster and with better style than we could on our high-tech machines. The fact that dolphins like to spend so much time in play is another sign of their intelligence – they need to keep their huge always-working brains stimulated. Luckily for us, we are big enough to fall into the category of plaything rather than dinner, so we could really appreciate these brilliant animals at close quarters in complete safety.

With awesome tactics, great speed, and its own hunting language, the Bottlenose Dolphin could actually be the most essential animal on the list!

Right Cute? Cuddly? Yes, but the Bottlenose Dolphin is also one of the most intelligent, organized and ultra-developed predators on the planet.

Tiger Snake

Notechis scutatus

Australians are very fond of boasting to tourists about the fact that they have more animals that could kill you than any other place in the world; I guess it's a kind of macho thing. Much as I hate to admit it, when it comes to snakes they are definitely right.

The most toxic venom of any snake belongs to Australia's Inland or Western Taipan, also known as the Fierce Snake. Its venom is about 10 times stronger than that of any other snake, and it should be able to kill a whole football team without breaking sweat (well, actually no snake ever sweats, but that's another story…).

In fact, this snake is anything but fierce, and nobody has ever been killed after a bite from one.

Tiger striped

One of the more fearsome snakes in Oz is the Tiger Snake, which possesses a stronger toxin than any snake found outside of Australia. This snake feeds almost exclusively on frogs, and like most of the Australian elapids (snakes in the cobra family) the venom is so potent that the snake can strike, withdraw, and wait, with no need to hold on to prey that could fight and do it damage. The deadly toxin works so fast that the prey doesn't have time to get more than a few metres away before it falls down dead.

The first place we went to look for Tiger Snakes was Herdsman's Lake, just on the outskirts of Perth. You could see the city skyline clearly from where we began searching in the long grass around the lake, joggers and cyclists were regularly going past us, and yet we were pulling SCORES of Tiger Snakes from the grass.

My aim was to prove that actually these 'monster snakes' are little or no danger to people. After all, the area was highly used, yet no one had ever been bitten there.

Smart snakes

The reason for this was obvious; get too close to a Tiger Snake and it will slither off into the grass at high speed. It can't eat you, so why would it bother to try to kill you if it doesn't have to?

The snakes we caught were just desperate to get away from us, which I demonstrated in dramatic style.

I caught one specimen and handled it for a few minutes until it was thoroughly annoyed, making a mini hood like a cobra, hissing and striking at me. I could see that all it really wanted was to escape, and I was so sure it just wanted shelter that I placed it on the ground, and knelt motionless while it slithered between my legs and off into the bushes.

It was a bit of a nervy moment, but I hope it shows perfectly how ill-understood snakes can be, and how genuinely predictable they are when you get to know them.

Even so, Tiger Snakes have got to make it onto the list for the strength of their venom alone. No snake outside of Australia has venom anything like as potent, and if you're a frog, you can forget it!

Left The stripes on this individual clearly show where the Tiger Snake gets its name from!
Below Handling snakes is very dangerous if you don't know what you're doing. Luckily, this one slithered off safely when I let him go.

Tiger Snake

SIZE:
XXX

SPEED:
XXX

WEAPONS:
XXXXX

DEADLY RATING:
XXXXX

Bluefin Tuna

Thunnus spp.

As a kid, I kind of figured that tuna were probably small, unremarkable fish that when squished up would just about fit into one of those little round tins you use for sandwiches. The first time I ever saw a wild one on a dive however, I remember it blocking out the sun.

Bluefin Tuna

SIZE:
✕✕✕

SPEED:
✕✕✕✕✕

WEAPONS:
✕

DEADLY RATING:
✕✕✕

It cruised past me like a languid torpedo, dropping its jaw and giving me an exaggerated yawn to display its teeth... it was clearly not to be trifled with. In fact, tuna have been caught that weigh as much as 10 men!

However, it's not just their size that's impressive; they have exquisite streamlining and muscle structure that allows them to be almost warm-blooded and keep up high speeds for uncommonly long periods of time. This is rare in cold-blooded fish. Blood that has been warmed up by the effort of swimming runs alongside cooler blood and heats it up. It's almost as if the fish's veins and arteries work like long thin radiators.

Finely tuna-ed

It's the shape of these fish that makes them such fearsome fighters. The body shape is slightly rounder and squatter than a missile designed to travel through air, perfect for powering through the water: the perfect fish torpedo!

When cruising at speeds of around 10 miles per hour, the fins extend outwards, making the fish amazingly manoeuvrable. When the tuna increase their speed they streamline their shape by folding the fins into slots to reduce drag.

All that remains are tooth-shaped finlets in front of the tail which help to stabilize the fish when they chase down prey at speeds of up to 40 miles per hour.

Beyond sandwiches

Seeing tuna feeding on a shoal of fish is one of the great spectacles of the natural world. However, thanks to our overwhelming desire to get tuna on the dinner table, it's increasingly rare to see these magnificent fish in the wild.

It's entirely possible that the only tuna the next generation will be able to see are those farmed in huge pens

out at sea. As if that weren't bad enough, many methods of tuna fishing are incredibly bad for other sea wildlife. Catching them in nets results in accidental 'bycatch' of dolphins, which enter the nets to follow the fish but cannot escape and then drown.

More recently, the practice of long-line fishing for tuna has been decimating the world's population of albatrosses and other large seabirds. When the birds try to take the bait from the long-line's many hooks they are dragged under the water and drowned.

Maybe it's time to try a different sandwich, for the sake of the amazing tuna and the other creatures of the deep ocean.

The Bluefin Tuna earns a place on our list for being the ultimate high-tech fish, its every detail precision-engineered for unbeatable underwater performance.

Right Biologists consider the tuna to be the height of fish evolution: a turbo-charged tuna torpedo!

Platypus

Ornithorhynchus anatinus

The famously weird 'Duck-billed Platypus' of Australia might be the most unlikely animal we went after on the whole series. It's a small, furry, egg-laying mammal that looks like a beaver with a duck's beak stuck comically on the front.

Platypuses can literally find food with their eyes closed. They forage on the riverbed in murky waters using electro-receptors on their bills to locate prey by detecting the tiny electrical pulses generated by their moving muscles. If you were a crayfish or a riverbed worm, you would undoubtedly find the Platypus a deadly danger. But it's not their exceptional foraging skill that gets these strange animals onto the Deadly 60.

It's the fact that the male Platypus is one of the very few venomous mammals in the world. At the base of the hind leg is a curved spur attached to a venom gland. The animals are said to use this spur when fighting with other males, especially during the breeding season. Although the venom they can inject won't kill a human it is said to induce some of the worst pain imaginable.

I'd filmed with Platypuses before, and found it almost impossible because they came to the surface for no more than a few seconds before diving again. For Deadly 60 we joined someone who needed to catch one for research and based ourselves at an Adelaide sanctuary with a healthy population of Platypuses.

We strung out a long net across a pond where they were most often seen and waited.

Newsworthy

Once a Platypus was in the net, we would have less than a minute to get to it before it was at risk of drowning, so it was all quite tense and nervous.

Unfortunately, we were not alone. A local news crew had turned up with all guns blazing to film us at work. They didn't know that you have to keep quiet when filming wildlife, and they chatted and laughed loudly at the side of the pond. There was no chance of a Platypus coming out.

A moment too late

Every half hour or so we'd ask them to be quiet, and they'd stage whisper for a few minutes. Unsurprisingly, not a single Platypus turned up. The first night we stayed out till about 1 AM before heading home and getting some rest. The owners of the sanctuary told us the Platypus came out just minutes after we left.

On the second night a Platypus finally appeared, but we never managed to catch it – or any other.

So I didn't get my wish to see a Platypus up close, but these bizarre animals still make it onto the Deadly 60 for their weirdness, their electrical sensors, and above all that remarkable venomous spur.

Left The venomous spur on the rear legs of the male Platypus is one of the weirdest features of this creature – perhaps the oddest animal on the planet!
Below The Platypus dives with its eyes closed. Visibility in the water where they live is usually so poor that good eyesight is pointless.

Platypus

SIZE:
✕✕✕

SPEED:
✕

WEAPONS:
✕✕✕

DEADLY RATING:
✕✕✕✕

Australian Giant Cuttlefish

Sepia apama

Every year for a month or so, the small seaside town of Whyalla in South Australia plays host to one of the world's great natural wonders. It's an event that was totally unknown even in the town itself till very recently, for the simple reason that it happens beneath the waves.

Here, with a giant industrial pier in the background and steelworks off behind, divers who enter the chilly waters are rewarded with a spectacle of extraordinary colour and bizarre animal behaviour. It is the largest known gathering on the planet of Australian Giant Cuttlefish.

The bright fantastic

Thousands, perhaps hundreds of thousands, of cuttlefish come together in these shallow waters to display, fight, mate and lay their eggs. Within seconds of entering the water we'd seen our first pairs getting close to each other. The males are much larger than the

Left Chromatophores (colour cells) beneath the skin of the cuttlefish, allow it to change colour faster than any other animal.
Right Not so bright now, are you?

SIZE:
XX XX

SPEED:
XX XX

WEAPONS:
XX XX XX XX XX

DEADLY RATING:
XX XX XX XX XX

females, and put on extreme displays to each other in order to scare off their rivals. The cuttlefish have the same sort of chromatophores (colour cells) as chameleons, but while a chameleon's colour change takes minutes, cuttlefish change instantly right before your eyes.

Not only can a cuttlefish change its whole body from white and pink to dark brown and purple in under a second, but it can also send pulsing waves of colour through its body, putting on its own miniature light show.

In battle, two big males will sidle up to each other, spreading their bodies widthways to make themselves bigger, flattening their eight tentacles alongside

their heads. They turn vibrant white with a purple and neon blue trim, then send waves of purple through the body, intimidating their opponent with their colours. All the while, the females huddle under a nearby ledge, adopting subtle orange and brown colours, rearing their tentacles up like sphinxes. They can also pinch their outer skin up in flaps to accentuate their camouflage. It's utterly remarkable.

Reflect on this

In order to demonstrate this behaviour to its best effect, I took down a huge mirror and showed a big male cuttlefish his own reflection.

He immediately assumed he was looking at another big bloke, and started showing off to... well, himself!

It was awesome. We even eventually got one hungry cuttlefish to strike a piece of fish out of my hand, which it did with perfect precision.

Dazzling stuff, but not especially deadly. However, there's more to these intelligent animals than flashy colours. They are skilful hunters of other sea animals, stalking their prey with tremendous care before launching an accurate, lightning-speed attack. At the same time, they are ever-ready to protect themselves from their own predators by using their amazing camouflage or firing a cloud of foul tasting, blinding black ink.

For me, the Australian Giant Cuttlefish was an absolute cert for the list.

Saltwater Crocodile

Crocodylus porosus

Throughout the filming of Deadly 60, director James and I spent many long car journeys discussing which animal should be at the top of the list. While I go to great lengths to big up various ants, snails and peculiar mammals, James always goes for the obvious: the Saltwater Crocodile.

Once found throughout Asia and Australasia, the 'saltie' is now threatened throughout much of its range due to habitat destruction and hunting – sometimes for its skin, sometimes simply because of fear. It's likely that most of the really huge monsters are gone and may not be seen again. However, in Australia they are protected and croc numbers are once again pretty healthy.

Man-eater

Of all the creatures we met that occasionally injure or kill people, I'm sure that the vast majority only hurt people when the animal is harassed or threatened, or it mistakes a human being for something else. This is not true of the saltie. It is one of the very few animals on earth which will deliberately hunt, kill and eat a human. If you enter its watery world you can expect to disappear in a brutal flurry of water and gore! We were in Australia's Northern Territory, where people have learned to keep well clear of water where crocs live. Someone is killed about every two or three years, but it's usually down to the victim being drunk and going down to the water's edge or even recklessly going for a swim in crocsville.

Occasionally, an individual croc can become a really significant threat to people, and it was just such a situation

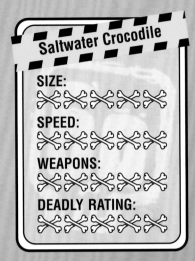

Saltwater Crocodile

SIZE:
✖✖✖✖✖✖

SPEED:
✖✖✖✖✖✖

WEAPONS:
✖✖✖✖✖✖

DEADLY RATING:
✖✖✖✖✖✖

that arose whilst we were in the Territory.

'Old Stinky' was a huge male who had evidently had a few run-ins with even huger crocs and had come off worse.

He had been pretty beaten up and was finding it difficult to hunt for his usual prey of fish and other aquatic animals, so he was getting closer and closer to fishermen on the riverbank. Local rangers thought it was only a matter of time before he took a chomp at one of them.

The night we went out to catch him, we saw his ruby red eyeshine just metres away from an unwise soul fishing at the riverside – totally unaware of the monster so close.

Sinking Old Stinky

The rangers approached close in a boat, dazzling Old Stinky with a flashlight before jabbing some short hooks into the bony scales behind his head and slipping a noose over his jaws. After a frantic fight, we hauled him up alongside the boat, and eventually got him up on shore, into a pick-up truck and off to spend the rest of his days in captivity, where

he couldn't cause any mischief! At least he would know where his next meal was coming from for the rest of his days.

At up to seven metres long full grown, with a bite that's probably the strongest in the animal kingdom, the saltie is a sure thing for the list.

Left That's one unlucky kangaroo!
Above Old Stinky would soon be unable to get into any more trouble. He's now being cared for in captivity.

Frilled Lizard

Chlamydosaurus kingii

Many of the animals in this book were on a 'hit list' that we set out to find from the word go, but we always tried to find time to look for any others that might qualify for the Deadly 60. 'Frillies' were very much in that category.

Frilled Lizard

SIZE:
✕✕✕✕

SPEED:
✕✕✕✕✕

WEAPONS:
✕✕✕

DEADLY RATING:
✕✕✕✕

Driving through the Kakadu National Park in Australia's Northern Territory, it was remarkable how often we saw fire – huge brush fires that raged for weeks on end and barbequed chunks of woodland the size of small countries. Many insects, frogs, lizards and small mammals have to flee the blaze, and predators have learned to take advantage of this. As you drive through the fires, the air above is not just thick with smoke, but also with kites and crows picking off scraps, and if you're very lucky you may just see a Frilled Lizard perched on a tree trunk, waiting for a meal to be flushed from the undergrowth.

Ashes to dashes

These lizards are 'sit and wait' hunters, lurking up trees in likely spots and waiting for the chance to grab a grasshopper, beetle or perhaps a smaller lizard. When they do spring into action they move amazingly fast, dashing down from their tree to grab the goodies.

Freshly burned ground is perfect for this hunting technique. The lizard's eyes are keen as a hawk's, but spotting the movement of a small creature is much easier on clear ground than when a layer of tangly grass and other vegetation is in the way.

It's the Frilled Lizard's scary threat display that has made it famous. Behind the head is a loose umbrella of skin, which can be erected in display to create the frightening image of a dragon far larger than the frillie actually is. It seems to work quite well – the only animals known to be brave enough to prey on Frilled Lizards are a few species of python.

If danger threatens and the dragon display hasn't worked, the lizard will make a run for it, beginning on all fours but then rising up to sprint off on its hind legs, frilled head bobbing about as it goes.

Freshly baked eggs

As with some other reptiles, the sex of the Frilled Lizard's offspring depends on the temperature at which its eggs are kept as the baby lizards develop inside.

The adults don't actually sit on their eggs to keep them warm, they bury them in damp earth for two or three months.

If the temperature in this underground nest is 29–36°C there will be equal numbers of males and females. Outside this range, either higher or lower, and more of the babies will be girls.

The baby lizards dig their way to freedom, and are able to rush about on two legs and display a mini frill from the day they are born.

The frillie was the inspiration for one of the dinosaurs in *Jurassic Park*, and although it's far smaller, and certainly not going to eat anyone, it definitely deserves to be included here!

Below One of the bravest and most peculiar reptiles in the world, the Frilled Lizard can even turn bush fires to its own advantage.

Ghost Bat

Macroderma gigas

Many people have a full-on phobia of them, but the vast majority of bats are vegetarian or eat only flying insects. Sure, there are some bats that spread rabies, and dung in their caves can transmit some pretty unpleasant diseases, but generally speaking bats are harmless. Well, harmless to humans.

Ghost Bat

SIZE:
✗✗

SPEED:
✗✗✗✗✗

WEAPONS:
✗✗✗✗

DEADLY RATING:
✗✗✗

The Ghost Bat – also known as the False Vampire Bat – is one of the few bats in the world that is not just an insect eater. It feeds on frogs, lizards, birds, and even other bats, using huge Dracula-like fangs to catch its unwary prey. Really huge bats are usually fruit bats but the Ghost Bat is a definite exception; it's the largest non-veggie bat in the world.

Going for gold

Our encounter with Ghost Bats took place in an abandoned gold mine in Australia's Northern Territory. We bent double to get through hot tunnels, going deeper underground, the walls running riot with thousands of huge cockroaches and spiders, the chirruping of the bats and beating of their huge wings drawing us towards the chambers where they roosted.

Their main chamber stank of the unmistakeable putrid smell of guano (another name for bat and bird poo) and every step was on 50 years' worth of poo, alive with shiny brown cockroaches. It was like an evil-smelling sauna, and made you want to puke with every breath. But the bats were worth the effort.

In our torchlight, their white fur and diaphanous wing membranes glowed like the tattered robes of phantoms, and their angry chattering at our presence made it feel even more like we were in a horror movie.

Phantom-tastic!

I had a net with me, and swished it twice into the air. On the second swing it bulged with a flapping bat.

Up close, the huge petal-like ears, twisted leaf-shaped nose and pointy canine teeth made for one of the weirdest faces I've ever seen, and one I'll not forget in a hurry.

As night fell, we sat outside in the entrance to the mines and watched these beasts fly out to hunt, flapping past our ears like flying hand towels...

You wouldn't want to be a smaller bat out there, with those demons chasing you!

Sound and vision

Like all hunting bats, Ghost Bats zero in on their prey using echolocation. They squeak constantly and the bounced-back echoes of the squeaks tell them about objects around them. Large stationary objects are steered around, and small moving objects are potential meals to pounce on. These bats are not as short-sighted as some other species, and they use sight as well as sound when they hunt.

When they've locked onto their prey, a quick dive and a single bite with those tremendous Dracula teeth finishes it off and the meal is then carried away to be eaten at leisure.

As bats go, they are about as fearsome as you could imagine. These creatures are the stuff of nightmares, and that's why they're on the list.

Below In the wing, you can see the fingers and joints of the bat's distinctly mammalian 'hand' – they're not so different from us after all!

Paralysis Tick

Ixodes holocyclus

People are always asking me if there are any animals I don't like, and ticks are certainly not among my favourites. Generally, however, these spider-like parasites are just a bit of a nuisance, getting up your trouser legs and sucking your blood if you wander through grass where livestock has been grazing.

In Australia, the effects can be much more than just irritating. The Paralysis Tick, a silvery-looking sucker no larger than a blackhead when not stuffed full of blood, has a toxin in its saliva that in even tiny quantities can prove lethal.

The tick latches on to warm-blooded animals, usually crawling to an exposed part of the body and wandering down to a warm place with a good blood supply, such as the groin or an armpit. It sinks in its fiercely sharp mouthparts, and blood begins to flow into its body.

Bloodsuckers

Like many parasites that take a blood meal, the tick's saliva contains anticoagulants (chemicals that stop blood from clotting). In this case, the saliva also contains a substance which can cause total paralysis after a few hours. It is only released by female ticks which are about to lay eggs, and it's most dangerous when the tick has been attached for five days or more. Male ticks bite and feed only rarely.

Our meeting with the Paralysis Tick began with a call to a local vet. Most reported bites affect livestock or domestic cats and dogs, which often don't recover when they are bitten.

This time, however, it wasn't an animal that had been bitten but an animal keeper. This fella ran a cow farm, and had a tick attached to his neck. It had only been there a few hours, but he already had a nasty headache. The vet removed the flea-sized monster, and we looked at it closely under a lens – seeing up close the evil-looking jaws and clinging legs.

Bat attack

Next, we went to an animal sanctuary whose owner specializes in rescuing just one kind of mammal – bats. There are three species of fruit bat or flying fox found in Queensland, and all of them pick up ticks when they drop to the ground to feed, bringing them back up to the treetop homes where they roost.

Mother bats are often paralysed by tick bites, and drop from their perches with babies still clinging to them. It's these little ones the sanctuary rehabilitates, and at peak times of year they can be bringing in 20 or 30 bats a week.

People have suggested that the tick toxin has evolved to prevent its prey from running away, but this doesn't make any sense to me. After all, if the prey dies, it's no further use to the tick, and no other blood suckers use this strategy.

I think it's just an unhappy accident of nature that makes the Paralysis Tick one of the most scary little suckers out there. It certainly puts it on the Deadly 60!

Left An invertebrate not much larger than a full stop that can kill a cow? I'd hate to tangle with this beastie! **Below** When mother fruit bats are paralysed by ticks they fall out of their treetop roosts. This little guy was rescued by a sanctuary after his mum was bitten.

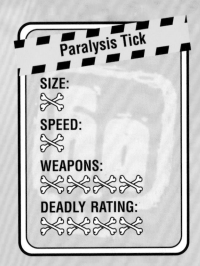

Paralysis Tick

SIZE:
✗

SPEED:
✗

WEAPONS:
✗✗✗✗✗

DEADLY RATING:
✗✗✗✗✗

43

Lace Monitor
Varanus varius

One of my colleagues in natural history is Dr Bryan Grieg Fry – perhaps *the* world expert in venoms. After surviving years of work with dangerous animals, he was savaged by one of his own pet Lace Monitors, which ripped through flesh, bone and tendons, and left his arm hanging on by a few threads.

Bryan is part of the University of Melbourne team who proved that monitor lizards such as Komodo Dragons, Perenties and Lace Monitors actually possess true venoms. His experience is testament to the awesome killing potential of the Lace Monitor, one of the largest monitor lizards in the world.

The bite stuff

It was always assumed that the only venomous lizards in the world are the Gila Monsters and Beaded Lizards, but Bryan's team based their studies on long experience of being bitten! After a munch from a Lace Monitor, humans experience rapid swelling within minutes, shooting pains and problems with blood clotting.

The related Komodo Dragons can kill prey as large

as a Water Buffalo. Even if they don't finish it off straight away, poisons in the saliva will kill the buffalo in a day or two.

Lace Monitors use their venom, along with their speed and raw power, to overwhelm prey such as insects, other reptiles, small mammals and birds. They also enjoy birds' eggs, and many have scars from violent encounters with Brush Turkeys, large birds which bury their eggs in warm piles of leaves, and vigorously defend these nests from intruders.

Monitoring the situation

I met my Lace Monitor at a picnic site in Australia, right close to the beach in the rainforest at Cape Tribulation. He was a magnificent beast, close to two metres in length, with dark green and olive mottled colours, and a swaggering gait that made it very clear *he* was king here, and my presence was supremely irrelevant. I crawled behind him on my belly so the cameraman could get us both in shot, but I got just a little too close for comfort – he whirled around in a flash and snapped at me,

before running up a vertical, featureless tree trunk as easily as if it were flat ground.

Later on, he came back down to ground level, and as I lay in the dry leaves he wandered right up to me, huge tongue flickering over my face and arms, tasting to see if I'd be good to eat. I have to admit I was a wee bit nervous to be face to face with this living dinosaur. With his vicious curved talons, a tail he could use as a whip-like weapon, and those fearsome teeth, I was in no doubt that he and his kind should be on the list.

Left and right Don't dismiss these 'dinosaurs'. Lace Monitors have been around for a long time because they're so good at hunting anything they can get their teeth into!

Lace Monitor

SIZE:
✕ ✕ ✕ ✕ ✕

SPEED:
✕ ✕ ✕ ✕

WEAPONS:
✕ ✕ ✕ ✕ ✕ ✕

DEADLY RATING:
✕ ✕ ✕ ✕ ✕

Redback Spider
Latrodectus hasselti

Australia is known for venomous spiders, and certainly has some of the most frightening in the world. The Redback is perhaps the scariest. Related to the notorious Black Widow Spider, it's not the largest nasty spider in Oz, but it is known for lurking unseen in outdoor toilets and outbuildings, and biting people unawares.

Redback Spider

SIZE:
✖✖✖

SPEED:
✖✖✖✖

WEAPONS:
✖✖✖✖✖

DEADLY RATING:
✖✖✖✖✖

Redbacks have a really horrid venom, called alpha-latrotoxin, which can do a lot of damage to people. The male's fangs are too small to puncture human skin (in most cases), but the females are larger and so are their teeth – most Redback bites are down to them.

The venom can kill an adult human but this is very unusual – children and elderly people are most at risk. Australian scientists have developed an antivenin, so nowadays Redbacks are seen as much less of a threat. There have been no deaths from bites reported since the antivenin was created in 1956.

Easy does it
In certain parts of Oz the Redback is very common, and I've come across these spiders often – certainly often enough to get the measure of what they're about.

My theory about the majority of animals is that they do not want to attack human beings. They just want to be left alone. I put this theory to the most intense test with the Redback, actually allowing one to wander over my hands. Though my heart was in my mouth the whole time, the spider never showed any sign of biting me, she just strolled over my hands, leaving a trail of silk as she went.

I'm content that my theory is safe, but please, please, please *don't* ever try it if you find a potentially dangerous animal – I do this for a living and there are always people on hand to help me if things go wrong!

Elastic entanglements
Although they possess such devastating venom, Redbacks still use webs to capture their prey like many of their less lethal relatives. However, they don't just catch flies. The webs are strong enough to entangle larger creatures, including crickets and even small lizards, and the spiders' venom does the rest.

These spiders also use their silk in even more remarkable ways. Redbacks will drag down long silken threads from their web and fix them to the ground. When small insects are unlucky enough to bump into these sticky elastic threads they become entangled and in their struggle they release the silky cord from its attachment. PING! The thread recoils and the insect is fired up into the air like a bungy jumper on the rebound! While the poor insect hangs there helplessly the spider can move in at leisure for a meal.

Crimes of passion

Redbacks are even deadly to each other – females usually eat the males during mating. In fact, the male spider often actually assists the female in his own destruction, somersaulting over as they mate so his abdomen is placed temptingly in front of her face. By laying down his life in this way, the male is more likely to successfully fertilize the female's eggs – the mating lasts longer when the female is busy eating her partner. So much for true love…

After mating, the female lays up to 300 eggs, which she keeps carefully in an egg sac – a silken cocoon that looks like a ping-pong ball.

Once the eggs have hatched, each tiny new spiderling hurls itself to the wind on the end of a silk parachute. Wherever the parachute lands becomes the spider's new home where it spins its first web.

For its rapacious ways, powerful venom and habit of lurking just where people are most likely to place their hands – or bottoms – the Redback earns its place on the list.

Above With its bungy jump web and powerful venom, this little spider is an insect's worst nightmare. This one is guarding two egg sacs, each containing hundreds of eggs.

Bengal Tiger

Panthera tigris

There are many animals on this list that will raise an eyebrow, but surely nobody is ever going to question the inclusion of the Bengal Tiger. This huge and powerful cat stealthily creeps up on its prey and then suddenly leaps out of nowhere in a fatal ambush.

When we were tracking tigers in India, we found scratch marks high up a tree where a tiger had stood on its hind legs and drawn its claws down the bark, like a domestic moggy using a scratching post. It looked as if someone had ripped a fistful of kitchen knives through the bark with the strength of three men!

Hidden treasure

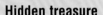

One of the great problems of natural history filmmaking is that some of the animals people are most used to seeing on TV are actually some of the hardest to find in the wild. All the tigers you've seen in adverts are tame and trained. Try and actually get close to one in the wild and you'll find it's a very different proposition.

Bengal Tigers are very rare — probably only about 1,500 are left in the wild in India. They have vast ranges, sometimes as much as 1,500 square kilometres, and are so well camouflaged that they could be five metres away and you would never see them. Searching for one is a bit like trying to find a straw-coloured needle in a haystack!

So we set aside our five days in India just to find a tiger.

We drove around searching constantly in freezing rain. On day two, we saw a tiger nose in and out of some bushes about 100 metres away, but that was it. On day five, as we faced up to the fact that we just weren't going to see one, everything suddenly changed.

First I found tracks and super-fresh tiger poo. Then we heard deer and monkeys making alarm calls in the bushes near us — a sure sign that a tiger was around. Then we heard our first roar; a deep guttural bellow that reverberated up through the ground and shook the fillings in our teeth.

Burning bright

When we finally found the tiger, a bunch of other people

had got there first. That, however, didn't spoil the moment as he sauntered across the road in front of us, his great shoulders rippling. He was a predator from head to toe, but it was quite a tame encounter. Well... it was tame until we thought it was over.

Just as we were about to pull our jeeps away, Jonny the cameraman realised that the tiger was actually still there right alongside the track.

We had inadvertently got too close and encroached on his space. In the blink of an eye, the mellow cat turned into the most fearsome thing I've ever seen. He lunged forwards roaring, his huge canine teeth flashing. The jeep was open-sided and he could have leaped right in and disembowelled Jonny before anyone was any the wiser.

Fortunately, the driver threw the jeep into reverse. The tiger baulked and withdrew and Jonny went flying on his backside – but not before filming the charge; ten seconds of TV gold for our first and fiercest feline!

Bengal Tiger

SIZE:
✕✕✕✕✕✕

SPEED:
✕✕✕✕✕✕

WEAPONS:
✕✕✕✕✕✕

DEADLY RATING:
✕✕✕✕✕✕

Below The moment we all thought cameraman Jonny was about to get munched. This fuzzy still from our TV camera shows just how close this leaping tiger came!

Gharial

Gavialis gangeticus

This would have to be the weirdest and most wonderful of all the crocodilians, but unlike the others, it's not on the list for the potential danger it poses to people. The Gharial is a fish-feeder *par excellence*, its tremendously long, slender snout working like a spiked trap for snaring prey.

This remarkable snout cuts through the water far more easily than the broader snout of an alligator or saltie. The teeth that poke out from the side of the mouth help the Gharial snag and snare fish that come close. Then it comes to the surface and chucks the fish down its gullet whole.

In the past it has had a reputation as a man-eater, but it's physically incapable of killing prey as large as a human, because the jaws are nothing like as powerful as those of other crocs. They are light and fast-snapping, which makes them more effective at catching lots of fish, rather than overloaded with crunch power like those of its beefier relatives. In fact, it's not uncommon to see the slightly surreal sight of a Gharial that is missing its upper jaw because the whole spindly thing has snapped off – possibly in a fight with another Gharial. This could never happen with the bulky bony jaw of another crocodilian. Amazingly, Gharials can survive

Left and above One of the most remarkable, and most threatened, animals on the list. The Gharial could soon be seen only in books.

for many years after losing half their fish-trapping jaws. It just goes to show what efficient fishermen they are.

Sandy situations

Like Nile Crocodiles, the female lays her eggs on the shore and covers them up with sand to keep them at a constant temperature, so Gharials need to have access to sandy river shores to breed. The mother protects her nest fiercely from any jackals, mongooses and other passing animals that might be interested in the eggs.

The Gharial is said to be the second largest croc, at up to six metres, but I reckon the Saltwater and Nile Crocodiles take first and second place, and the Gharial comes in third. The dubious honour it probably does have is that of being the rarest crocodilian. It used to be found in deep, fast-flowing rivers across the Indian subcontinent but is now extinct everywhere except India and Nepal, where it is very rare – estimates suggest there may be as few as 200 adult breeding pairs alive today. It is classified as critically endangered, and it wouldn't take much to remove this magnificent animal from the planet altogether.

A losing battle?

Why is it in so much trouble? Habitat loss as people farm the land right up to the river bed is destroying the Gharial's breeding places; and the animals are also killed by people – either accidentally (by getting caught up in fishing nets) or deliberately (by fishermen who don't like the idea of sharing the river with these skilful fish-catchers). Pollution of the rivers is another threat.

Like the other animals in this book, the Gharial is a brilliantly sophisticated hunter, beautifully adapted to its lifestyle. Unfortunately, that's not always enough when people are destroying animal habitats with wanton disregard and at a frighteningly rapid rate.

Conservation groups are struggling to keep the Gharial from becoming another extinction statistic and it's a tough battle. It earns a place on the list for now; let's hope it stays there for years to come.

Gharial

SIZE:
✕✕✕✕✕

SPEED:
✕✕✕

WEAPONS:
✕✕✕✕✕

DEADLY RATING:
✕✕✕✕

Asian Elephant
Elephas maximus

I hadn't considered putting the Asian Elephant on the list. After all, they're supposed to be total pussycats next to African Elephants, and the first time we saw them on this trip they came closer to our jeep than I would ever think of getting to an African Elephant.

In fact, I had been thinking of choosing bee-eaters (graceful insect-catching birds) as the next contender. However, as we were coming out of the forest at the end of day five looking for tigers, we happened upon a large herd of elephants coming out of the bushes towards us. We slowed a little to allow them to pass – a

mistake, it turned out, as the matriarch (the head female elephant)was obviously extremely highly strung.

The group had some calves around, which often tends to make the adults a bit twitchy, and they were probably feeling pretty territorial.

Charge of the heavy brigade
Even so, it was still a shock when this monstrous female charged at us, trumpeting furiously. She was no more than a metre away from Nick our sound recordist (in the back of the jeep) when our driver realised what was happening and stomped on the gas.

The jeep pulled away, but she wasn't stopping! She chased after us as we sped off, raging her intent to smash us into bits.

I'm sure that many people who've seen these animals in the wild will think I'm full of it. Indeed, all the charges I've had from African Elephants have been mock charges – they storm up close flapping their ears and making a right racket, but pull up short. It's just a big show to frighten you. I don't think this Asian Elephant had that intention. She simply wanted to smash us.

As she probably weighed five tonnes, and could have tossed our jeep right over, I really think we had a very, very close call.

Even more so because after the incident was over, we'd got away safely and the elephant was no longer a danger to us, we stopped the jeep and then tried to start it again...The engine was as dead as a dodo.

Gentle giants?

Asian Elephants are tamed and used as a beast of burden in many countries, and they are much praised for their intelligence and gentle nature.

Their unique combination of braininess and massive strength has made them extremely useful for a wide range of tasks, from timber-carrying to warfare.

Indian mahouts (elephant drivers) often establish an incredibly close relationship with their animals, and it can last a lifetime – elephants live as long as people.

However, you'd be very unwise not to respect the animal's sheer size and strength. Upset a female with a calf, or get in the way of a male who's in 'musth' (a kind of frenzy that affects male elephants for a few days each year) and you could very easily get trampled to pieces.

For strength, size, and aggression defending their young or personal space, the Asian Elephant is an unexpected entrant on the Deadly 60.

Above The moment Asian Elephants became a contender for the list. This large lady was obviously intent on taking out her rage on our jeep, and on us!

Asian Elephant

SIZE:
✕✕✕✕✕✕

SPEED:
✕✕

WEAPONS:
✕✕✕

DEADLY RATING:
✕✕✕

Praying Mantis

Mantis religiosa

There is a story in Chinese kung fu about a Shaolin monk who was watching a Praying Mantis hunt one day. The mantis was being approached by a much larger insect, perhaps hoping to have the mantis for lunch, but the mantis stayed completely still, right up until the second the predator was about to pounce...

Praying Mantis

SIZE:
✗

SPEED:
✗ ✗ ✗ ✗ ✗

WEAPONS:
✗ ✗ ✗

DEADLY RATING:
✗ ✗ ✗ ✗

Then suddenly with lightning speed the mantis struck its potential attacker, killing it instantly with a blow from the powerful forelegs that moments ago were held up as if in prayer.

The Shaolin monk was so impressed that he developed an entire style of kung fu based around the awesome killing power of the mantis.

Among the ants

There are about 2,000 species of mantis found worldwide, mostly in warm climes. Some of them grow to as long as a fountain pen, and are capable of drawing blood from a human hand.

It's the tinier mantises, though, that really catch my attention. Searching the bushes in India, the first ones I found were masquerading as ants.

Ants are nasty biting and stinging fiends, and very few animals will mess with them. In fact, some mantises mimic ants to avoid being eaten when they're still nymphs (babies).

Making baby mantises is a dangerous job – for the father at least. Although he performs a courtship display to distract the female and get her thinking about romance rather than lunch, it doesn't always work, and the female may well grab and devour him after mating if he isn't careful.

The male is able to tell whether his intended mate has recently eaten or if she is feeling hungry. If it's the latter, he will approach her very carefully and beat a hasty retreat when it's all over.

The female lays up to 400 eggs in a single frothy mass, which hardens to form a tough, protective case around the eggs. In some species, the female guards this egg case, but in most she leaves it to take its chances.

Masters of disguise

Many of the larger mantises have some of the most extraordinary methods of camouflage in nature, disguising themselves as dead leaves, tree bark, dried grass or even as the most beautiful orchid flowers.

Whatever costume they're wearing, the reason these remarkable beasts make it onto the list is the same for all of them. They have perhaps the most sophisticated eyes in the insect world, with compound lenses made up of tens of thousands of units, covering most of the head and giving near 360° vision.

Though insects' eyes may not see shapes as clearly as we do, they are much better at spotting movement. That's one reason why it's so hard to swat a housefly!

As well as awesome visual capabilities, the mantis has fiercely barbed forearms, used to strike at and catch its prey – usually soft-bodied flying insects such as butterflies.

Lastly, it has an ear that runs along the underside of the body, which is excellent at picking up the sonic tones bats make as they hunt. If a mantis hears a bat approaching, it will often fold its wings and drop into the leaf litter, where the bat cannot find or catch it.

The mantis is the scourge of the insect world, a miniature master at mincing moths, and definitely on the Deadly 60.

Below Small but perfectly formed, are the praying mantises the finest invertebrate hunters on our list?

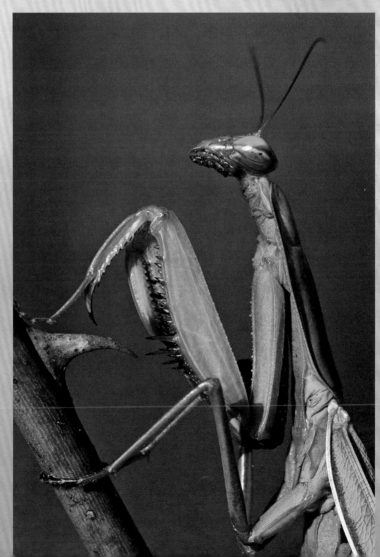

King Cobra

Ophiophagus hannah

Whenever people ask me what my favourite animal is, I usually bore them for an hour while coming up with no real answer at all. Ask what my favourite snake is though, and it's easy. The King Cobra is without question the most impressive, the most intelligent and the most terrifying snake on the planet.

Let's start with the stats. The King Cobra, or Hamadryad, is the longest venomous snake on the planet with a record length of 5.6 metres. It can hold a third of its body length off the ground when hooded and erect – so a huge King can stand and look a grown man in the eye. It is the only snake that builds a nest for its young. It feeds only on other snakes, injecting so much venom in each bite that in theory it could kill an elephant – or 20 men. It's said that a bite direct to an artery could be fatal to a human within two minutes.

Don't sit on the King
Convinced? You should be! The first time I saw a King Cobra in the wild was in Sumatra. I was out trekking in the jungle,

dumped my sack on the ground and went to sit down on a fallen log. As I approached, a King that had been curled up there reared up, towering over me and hissing like an alien from a movie. I'm not too proud to admit that I backed away and ran for it!

Many years later, I managed to handle a King Cobra in the wild for the first time. It was a huge beast, perhaps 3.5 or 4 metres long, and as I approached, it started to disappear up a tree.

Desperate not to let my prize escape, I clambered up after it, and found myself clinging onto the tail of the largest venomous snake in the world, while it turned towards me roaring in anger. It was the most frightening animal encounter I've ever had.

A bad press?

The King Cobra is unique in the intelligence it shows, and the complexity of its social life.

Males will fight over their mates, trying to pin each other to the ground to gain the upper hand and win the bride. Once the courtship and mating has taken place, the female lays eggs in a nest she has made out of leaves.

She'll then stand guard over the nest until the young have hatched and moved away. This is really unusual — in fact, no other species of snake does it.

Like all cobras, if a King is threatened it will stand up, expand its hood and hiss. Due to special membranes in the back of the King's throat the hiss is almost more like a growl!

Other snake species can be easily distracted by a swaying snake hook or other object, but the intelligent King Cobra will disdainfully ignore the distraction and look you straight in the eyes.

It rarely if ever has to make a strike because very few attackers would be stupid enough to hang around when confronted with such obvious dominance!

Last but not least, the King Cobra feeds on other snakes, including the most venomous. It's truly the ruler of the serpents.

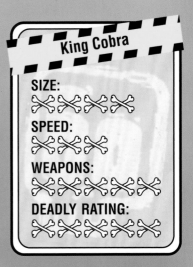

King Cobra

SIZE:
☠ ☠ ☠ ☠

SPEED:
☠ ☠ ☠

WEAPONS:
☠ ☠ ☠ ☠ ☠ ☠

DEADLY RATING:
☠ ☠ ☠ ☠ ☠ ☠

Left An adult King Cobra can be three times as long as I am tall, can stand up to look a fully grown man in the eye, can growl rather than just hiss and has enough venom to kill an elephant… any questions!?

Sloth Bear
Melursus ursinus

I have to admit, including the Sloth Bear was director Rosie's idea – to me they were just big bumbling furry clowns that really didn't deserve consideration. How wrong I was! In the wild, they are known for being short-sighted, unpredictable beasts, decidedly grumpy if anyone approaches them when they have youngsters.

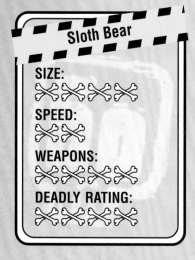

Sloth Bear

SIZE:
✕✕✕✕✕

SPEED:
✕✕

WEAPONS:
✕✕✕✕

DEADLY RATING:
✕✕✕✕

They have gargantuan scimitar-shaped claws which they use for tearing open bees' nests and termite mounds, and canine teeth that would put an Alsatian to shame. However, they do look incredibly comical, with floppy slobbering lips for slurping up honey, and bushy black hairdos. They can climb trees with ease and even hang upside-down from branches – hence the 'sloth' part of the name. Another name for the species is Honey Bear, because they are so fond of honey and other sweet foods.

Tiger of the bear world?

As we know, a sugary diet doesn't necessarily lead to a sweet temperament. Despite their dozy looks, Sloth Bears are big, powerful animals, and are often regarded as being more dangerous than tigers, which share their jungle habitat in India. Although tigers can and do kill Sloth Bears, the bears' unpredictable nature makes them potentially more dangerous to people. They attack in a haphazard but devastating way, using their huge teeth and claws to tear wildly at their victim's face and body. One particularly alarming individual killed 12 people before it was finally shot by the famous Indian hunter Kenneth Anderson.

Maybe the Sloth Bears are right to be annoyed with people though, for they have suffered unbelievably over the centuries at the hands of man.

On the streets of India, dancing bears have been used for generations to entertain tourists. The bears are taken from their parents at a very young age, have their teeth pulled out and a rope pushed through gaping holes drilled in their snouts. They then live a humiliating, painful life on the streets. Thankfully, this practice has now been declared illegal, and the dancing bears of India are finding their way to sanctuaries, such as the marvellous one in Agra where we had our incredible Sloth Bear encounter.

Domestic violence

My plan was to enter an enclosure with some of the bears and get to know them, but first we watched another enclosure where four bears had just been let in to feed. They spent a while galumphing about comically, making me think I'd been right, and they were going to be the most unworthy animal on the list. But then in a blink of an eye it all changed. It turned out one of the females was on heat, and she and two male bears just went crazy. In a swirling, roaring, screaming whirl of teeth and claws, they started trying to tear each other to shreds. It was utterly terrifying as the air filled with dust as the three animals went for each other with horrifying force and aggression.

The keepers wanted to intervene and stop serious injury, but to have entered the enclosure at that point would have meant certain death. The horror went on for about five or six minutes – just when you thought they had had enough, they'd go back at it again, with their huge canines flashing and claws ripping chunks of hair out of each other. As you can imagine, when I finally entered the enclosure, it was with my heart thumping like a big bass drum and I no longer had any doubt that the Sloth Bear should make the list!

59

Below This one looks soft and cuddly but you should always keep your distance from a wild Sloth Bear.

Wrinkle-lipped Bat

Tadarida plicata

Gomantong Cave, a network of underground tunnels and chambers in the north of Borneo, is one of the most unpleasant, most repugnant and most scary places that I've ever visited but I've had to go there several times now for filming. The reason?

Well, I've been there to find the Wrinkle-lipped Bats that inhabit Gomantong – and have done for centuries.

They have created huge mounds of poo below them, and this guano is just *alive* with flesh-eating cockroaches, highly venomous centipedes, assassin bugs and lots of other nasties.

It's also very squishy, and we sank knee-deep in the disgusting stuff as we made our laborious way into the depths of the cave.

Poop and soup

The bats share the caves with some remarkable birds: the edible-nest swiftlets. You've probably heard of birds' nest soup – well, it really *is* made out of birds' nests. The swiftlets' nests are tiny cups

which the birds construct out of their own saliva. Yes, birds' nest soup is really birds' spit soup. Nevertheless, it's considered a delicacy in many places, and licensed collectors take their lives in their hands and climb up wobbly bamboo poles to gather the nests from the steep cave walls. They follow strict rules to make sure that the nests are not over-harvested.

High-tech hunting

The bats of these caves are certainly worthy of inclusion on our list of fierce feeders. Around two million of them live here, and every evening they head out to eat several tonnes of insects from the surrounding forests.

They are astoundingly well adapted to catch insects, sending out a constant stream of little ultrasonic clicks which bounce back off their flying prey. This creates a radar-like image for the bats, which swoop in and snatch the helpless insects. Flies and moths don't stand a chance!

The bats need to eat often to give themselves enough energy to keep their tiny bodies warm and to fly, so they hoover up little winged creatures practically non-stop from dusk 'til dawn.

They start to leave the cave at about dusk, pouring out from the mouth of the cavern and from unseen holes and crevices in the rock walls.

This is about the same time that the swiftlets come home for the day, so birds of prey like kites and Serpent Eagles come to the entrance of caves to grab an easy meal from the whirling mass of fluttering bodies.

In order to get in amongst the waves of bats as they dropped off their ledges and headed out into the evening, I climbed way up into the roof of the cave, over 100 metres above the stinky dung beneath.

We'd set up a portaledge (a canvas sleeping platform that hangs on the rockface) and I sat inside it as the endless stream of bats poured past me, on their way to make life hell for the flying insects of Borneo.

The Wrinkle-lipped Bats earn themselves a place on the list because of their amazing

Wrinkle-lipped Bat

SIZE:
✕✕

SPEED:
✕✕✕✕✕

WEAPONS:
✕✕✕

DEADLY RATING:
✕✕✕

insect-catching powers, and also because of their sheer overwhelming numbers. They're just like a huge squadron of flycatching fighter pilots. More impressive than insecticide any day!

Left Any animal that hunts mosquitoes and midges is a friend of mine! With huge teams of super-sensed individuals leaving their bat cave to hunt every night, Wrinkle-lipped Bats are insect murderers *par excellence*!

Scutigera

Scutigera spp.

The scutigeras are the spookiest animals on earth – fact! There are thought to be about 100 species of these long-legged centipedes, most of them found in tropical environments around the world. Some are uniquely adapted to hunting in the dark, including those that live in Borneo's Gomantong caves.

Some scutigeras come out after night falls to hunt for their insect prey, but more often these centipedes will spend their whole life in the dark, in a cave or hollow tree.

One species of scutigera is the House Centipede, which is native to the Mediterranean and has spread around the world, although it is still very rare in Britain. This animal is about four centimetres long, with a frill of long legs on which it can rocket around at a startling speed. Its preferred quiet dark place is a cool corner of your house or maybe in the garden shed. Despite its scary appearance it is a good animal to have around, as it will keep houses free of cockroaches, flies, and other unwelcome insects.

Modified monsters

The type of scutigera we found in the Gomantong caves was much bigger, at 10 centimetres long or more, and much scarier than the House Centipede. As with most centipedes, the scutigeras' two front legs have become modified into venom-injecting claws. A nip from a House Centipede results in a sore bump, like a bee sting. With the monster scutigera of Borneo, this venom is dangerous enough to hospitalize a fully grown human. Just the week before we arrived at the cave system, a local worker was bitten and spent three days in hospital in extreme pain.

Versatile hunters

A scutigera hunts using its spindly long legs to feel around in the darkness like a blind man with his white stick. I've watched these remarkable hunters dangle their legs in the air, and when a passing moth brushes past them they'll snap it out of the air like lightning.

They can also race after their quarry at tremendous speed. The scutigera of Gomantong are spoilt for choice when it comes to prey; with a moving carpet of cockroaches and dung beetles eating all that bat and bird poo, the scutigera can grab a meal whenever they feel like it.

It's their speed of movement, and how they look as they move, which really sets them apart as the world's creepiest critter – that crippling dose of venom is just a bonus. With their 15 pairs of scuttling legs, they are absolute horrors, exactly the kind of creatures you'd expect to find in the dark caves of your worst nightmares, and that's why they're on the list.

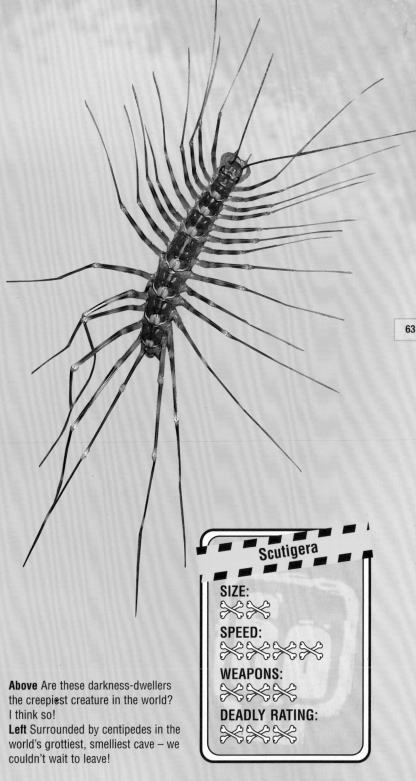

Above Are these darkness-dwellers the creepiest creature in the world? I think so!
Left Surrounded by centipedes in the world's grottiest, smelliest cave – we couldn't wait to leave!

Scutigera

SIZE:
☠☠
SPEED:
☠☠☠☠☠
WEAPONS:
☠☠☠☠
DEADLY RATING:
☠☠☠

Reticulated Python
Python reticulatus

Imagine a snake as long as five men lying head to toe on the ground. A snake capable of eating a pig, and then having an eight-month snooze! Imagine a snake with as many as 200 curved, pin-sharp teeth, which has been reported as having killed and eaten human children. You are imagining the Reticulated Python.

Whatever the truth of the tales about big snakes eating people, there is no doubt that the Reticulated Python of Asia is one of the world's most spectacular beasts, and it is certainly capable of killing a human.

It is probably the world's longest snake, although the Green Anaconda of South America is a strong contender for the title, and it's certainly heavier. The longest reliable measurement for a Reticulated Python was a staggering 9.74 metres. That snake was caught in Indonesia in 1912. Recently, a zoo in Indonesia has claimed to have a 15-metre long specimen. This last claim seems unlikely, and the zoo won't let anyone in to measure it...

Looking for the big one

My greatest almost-encounter with a Reticulated Python in the wild was a near miss in northern Borneo. We were following up a lead in a local palm plantation that a giant 'retic' had been munching its way through the workers' chickens and dogs. When I turned up there, they told me stories of seeing the snake crossing the road, and not being able to see either end of it, as its head was in the bushes on one side, and its tail in bushes on the other! We were directed to an ancient tribal burial ground called Elephant Rock; local people were afraid to go anywhere near the place because of the huge snake.

When we arrived, we found ancient ironwood coffins and old skulls, but also great sheets of snake skin which the creature had shrugged off when it last moulted, and rocks that were worn smooth by the passage of a truly gigantic snake. I first climbed deep into caves within the rock, my heart beating as if trying to jump clear out of my chest, but I found nothing. We staked out Elephant Rock for three nights, sitting in the darkness for hours on end hoping the snake would come and show itself, but it never did.

Snakes alive

On the last day, just as we were set to leave the area, we were called by one of the workers. A big snake had come into his garden and taken one of his chickens, before making a break for it. They had the snake holed up under a nearby bridge. I managed to catch it – although the four-metre beast was certainly a handful – and we took it to a local nature reserve to stop the locals killing it.

Though we did succeed in finding a *fairly* big snake, it was certainly not the same snake that we had been waiting to see. I'll always look back to Elephant Rock, and wonder about the beast that lives there... The idea of the impossibly giant snake is as exciting as ever, and that's why it's on the list.

Left Any snake that can munch down a wild boar deserves respect!

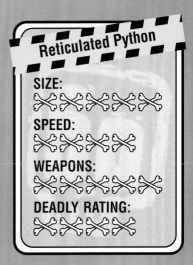

Reticulated Python

SIZE:
✕✕✕✕✕✕

SPEED:
✕✕✕✕✕

WEAPONS:
✕✕✕✕✕✕

DEADLY RATING:
✕✕✕✕✕

Mantis Shrimp
Order Stomatopoda

Having spent most of my life chasing wildlife, I've been lucky enough to see some amazing wildlife spectacles, whilst others I have chased for years and never quite managed to get. Mantis shrimp were among those right at the top of my wishlist… until we arrived in Borneo's Sipadan Island.

It may seem crazy to get so excited about a shrimp, but trust me, this must be one of the most exciting creatures on the planet. They are not closely related to true shrimps, and apart from a similar general shape, they're not shrimp-like at all — check out the great barbed claws, and their constantly moving stalked eyes that can see infrared and ultraviolet light as well as everything in between — no other animal has eyes like that.

Box clever

Broadly speaking, there are two main kinds of mantis shrimp: spearers and boxers. The Peacock Mantis is a boxer, with a pair of sturdy leg-like structures called palps at the front of its body, which it uses to punch its way through the shells of marine snails. The punch is powerful enough to smash right through bulletproof glass!

This is no joking matter; scuba divers call the Peacock Mantis 'split thumbs' because too many divers have got too close to these exotic-looking invertebrates and been thoroughly boxed!

The mantis shrimps I wanted to try and film were spearers. Shrimp is probably the most inappropriate name imaginable for them. They're never going to end up in a prawn cocktail!

They dig vertical burrows in the sand, and lie inside, just their eyes showing. However, when you dangle a piece of bait in front of them, they emerge from their burrows like an immense alien.

Spears of a clown

Some of them are the size of my lower leg, and poised beneath their carapace are two arms just like those of a praying mantis (hence the name). They slowly approach to within inches of their prey, then snap their arms out at a speed too fast for the eye to see.

Brutal barbs on the underside of these arms hook into the food, and in the blink of an eye the monster is gone, disappearing with its skewered dinner deep into a burrow that seems to disappear into the bowels of the sea bed. I managed to get many of these beasts to feed right from a stick in my hand, and it was more impressive than seeing a lioness take out a gazelle on the African plains!

One of the fastest movements in the animal world, and a surprisingly intimidating appearance, puts mantis shrimps way up there on my Deadly 60.

Mantis Shrimp

SIZE:
✖

SPEED:
✖✖✖✖✖

WEAPONS:
✖✖✖✖✖

DEADLY RATING:
✖✖✖✖

Left A stealthy Spear Mantis. If I'd got too close to its barbed arms my hands could have been sliced!

Below The pretty Peacock Mantis can punch through bulletproof glass. DO NOT TOUCH!

Chevron Barracuda

Sphyraena qenie

Sipadan Island is known as one of the finest diving destinations in the world, sitting in the South China Sea just north-east of Borneo. It's been a marine reserve for many decades now, which means everything is protected from fishing and is pretty much as nature intended.

Chevron Barracuda

SIZE:
XXX

SPEED:
XXXXXX

WEAPONS:
XXXXX

DEADLY RATING:
XXXX

Because diving is a very unpredictable game, there were very few animals we set out to try to film; you just never know what is going to turn up. The tropical reef is so alive with predators and toxic terrors that we knew we'd find some truly astounding stuff whatever happened.

However, even my expectations were totally surpassed this time.

Everything went dark

We'd been diving all day in bright clear sunshine, with visibility underwater of over 50 metres, which is so good it's crazy. It kind of feels like you're not diving in water at all but flying in air; the clearness of the water makes everything weird. However, in the afternoon, a cloud suddenly fell over everything, and the underwater world went dark.

Looking upwards from about 30 metres down, I gradually became aware that the cloud was not above the water but within it, between me and the surface. Though it blocked out the sun, it wasn't really grey, but a shimmering, living wall of silver.

It was a colossal shoal of Chevron Barracuda, the wolves of the ocean. Barracudas are sleek, streamlined fish, but powerfully built, with big shining eyes and long jaws packed with unbelievable teeth. They hunt other fish, using an incredible turn of speed to chase them down. By night they leave the shoal and head out over the reef, eating everything in their path.

Sometimes small groups will band together and cooperate to force their prey into shallower water, where it's more easy to catch. This 'pack hunting' habit is why they are compared to wolves.

If a barracuda has already eaten but happens upon another tasty-looking shoal of small fish, it may round them up and stand guard over them until it's ready to feed again. During the day, barracudas hang apparently motionless in the current, killing time until it's killing time!

Flashy fish

I swam up into the midst of the shoal, and then became a part of one of the most beautiful experiences I've ever had underwater. The barracudas — and there were thousands of them — began to swim in a perfect circle called a 'vortex', their bodies gleaming as the circle started spinning around and around… and I was right in the centre of them. It was amazing, one of the most stunning things I've ever seen.

There have been stories of barracudas attacking people, but despite their wicked gnashers and impressive size (some species grow to two metres or more) they are not people-eaters. As well as hunting for their own food, they sometimes follow larger underwater predators in the hope of scavenging the remains of a kill. It's possible that this is why they sometimes follow scuba divers.

The attacks that have happened were probably the result of the barracuda mistaking a flashing watch on a moving arm for the glinting scales of a fish. So they're not much of a risk to us, but their fearsome hunting ability gets them on the list for sure!

Above Lost in a vortex of Barracuda. This must surely be one of the ocean's most divine sights.

Lionfish

Pterois volitans

The Lionfish of the tropical Pacific Ocean is the dazzling showman of the reef. Like a Samurai warrior it stalks the coral heads looking for a fish supper, its waving array of huge colourful fins extended to herd fish before it like sheep.

Lionfish

SIZE:
✕✕✕

SPEED:
✕✕✕✕✕

WEAPONS:
✕✕✕✕✕

DEADLY RATING:
✕✕✕✕✕

The fins, which are separated into slim, waving fingers, conceal an array of spines, and at the base of each of those spines is a venom gland. Any diver unlucky enough to get spiked with one can expect excruciating pain. A hospital visit will be required, although the sting is rarely fatal.

Although usually a laid-back character, the Lionfish can be aggressive and will turn on anyone who gets too close, fins and spines aimed menacingly forwards.

Lion taming

Male Lionfish become very short-tempered with each other around mating time. Each male tries to court several females and if another male comes along while this is going on, the original male will attack him ferociously, trying to bite or spike him. Although they rarely kill each other, a spike with a spine means a dose of venom which apparently results in some pain and distress and the intruder will be savaged relentlessly until he backs down.

The venom is really only a defence mechanism, not used when feeding, and it was the Lionfish's abilities as a hunter that I wanted to see. These fish come alive at night, and large numbers of them were soon hunting around the lights of the jetty near where we were staying.

The lights attracted plankton, which in turn attracted larger fish, and the Lionfish were there to eat them. The smaller baitfish had no idea quite how much trouble they were in...

Sneaking up slowly

It was a fearsome sight. Despite the Lionfish being so brightly coloured and obvious to human eyes, they move slowly, fins spread out and pushed forward, and their bodies very still apart from the tail which beats gently, propelling them forwards. It's as if the smaller fish just don't see them at all. The fanned-out fins seem to block the prey's view of the

Lionfish's swishing tail, so they don't realise the lion is inching closer. I found myself shouting at the little fish to 'look out!' as the predators spied them and moved ever so easily towards them, before snapping the fish up with an audible 'pop!'. They were so accurate and so lethal that it was hypnotic to watch.

Lionfish have also been seen hunting small fish in another ingenious way. When predators approach, fish may jump out of the water to try to escape and to put some distance between themselves and the hunter. Lionfish sometimes watch jumping fish and position themselves to catch them when they fall back into the water.

They also rustle their spines as they swim slowly along, in the hope that the sound will entice curious prawns and other sea animals out of their burrows to be grabbed.

Deadly venom, super-fast strikes, a selection of special hunting skills and an enormous appetite – the Lionfish is a sure thing on the Deadly 60 list.

Below This ninja in striped pyjamas has vicious venom and a deadly strike to rival any animal on the list.

Gannet

Morus bassanus

Off the western coast of Wales, daily tides rage into the bay with such force that grade IV whitewater is created right there in the sea. The waves rip across submerged pinnacles that have claimed so many ships that they are known as 'The Bitches'. In order to get close to this Deadly 60 contender, we would have to paddle right through them and out to an exposed rock 11 miles out to sea. We were seeking some of the most lethal living harpoons on the planet, about 32,000 pairs of them, huddled together on Grassholm Island.

The magnificent sight of Gannets feeding has been named as Britain's most splendid wildlife spectacle, and with good reason. Britain's largest seabird, an adult Gannet has snowy white plumage, wingtips that look as though they are tipped with black molasses, Egyptian kohl eyeliner emphasizing the eyes, and a head that's been dipped in butterscotch. They fly on stiff wings, and circle about the skies of Grassholm dwarfing the Fulmars, Kittiwakes and Puffins that share their nest sites. Beautiful as they are, it's when they begin to hunt they really earn their deadly status.

Bomber patrol

When Gannets spot fish close to the surface, they will soar up to 40 metres above the sea, before banking sideways, fixing their prey with phenomenal eyesight, then folding their wings to their sides and plummeting like a torpedo. Hitting the water at around 60 miles per hour, they pierce the water's surface and spear their prey, or swim deeper down to snatch at the helpless fish. If a large shoal of fish is spotted, Gannets will begin dive-bombing them in sequence, tens or even hundreds of white arrows spearing fish beneath.

Water can be yielding and soft, but as anyone who's tried the high diving board at their local pool will know, if you hit the surface from a height it's like crashing into concrete.

Gannets — diving repeatedly from the height of a 10 storey building — are protected by pockets of air in the breast which cushion the vital organs much like airbags in a car. Unlike most birds, they must breathe through their mouths because they have no external nostrils. This prevents water entering their bills at high speed and blasting their brains out the back of their heads!

Wild at heart

For me, Gannets are a symbol of the wilderness. They only nest far from people on the most remote and isolated of sea islands, and so even the sight of one Gannet gives me the satisfaction of knowing I'm in the wilds. The black skies and raging rains that bombarded us as we struggled through The Bitches turned to blue skies and sunshine as we approached Grassholm, and our Deadly heroes. It was truly a day blessed by the gods of nature, for as we headed back to land, with Gannets circling overhead, a pod of Common Dolphins raced alongside coming close enough to touch, and the most exquisite rainbow I have ever seen hugged the Pembrokeshire coast. It was one of those days where there is nowhere in the world I would rather be than the glorious UK.

Gannet

SIZE:
✕✕✕

SPEED:
✕✕✕✕

WEAPONS:
✕✕✕✕

DEADLY RATING:
✕✕✕✕

73

Left 'Airbags' in the Gannet's chest protect the vital organs from massive impact when the bird hits the water.
Below Don't be fooled by that innocent white plumage, this bird is a cold-blooded killer. Gannets are avian dive-bombers without equal.

Common Otter

Lutra lutra

When Gannets were named as Britain's number one wildlife spectacle, the nation's favourite mammal was revealed as the Otter. It's easy to see why. When I was a child they were my most beloved creature – the adorable whiskered face and impossibly cute whistles and squeaks they make when chatting to each other, and the cubs' love of play as they slide down mudbanks and gleefully roll all over each other clearly happy to be alive. These most bewitching, beguiling and beautiful of beasts are inviting a good cuddle. Aren't they?

Common Otter

SIZE:
XXXX

SPEED:
XXXXX

WEAPONS:
XXXXX

DEADLY RATING:
XXXXX

Well, actually no. Otters are members of a group of animals that crops up repeatedly on the Deadly 60: the mustelids, or weasel family. In the UK they're represented by weasels, stoats, polecats, badgers, Pine Martens and the non-native American Mink. Worldwide, you can include vicious Honey Badgers and Wolverines in the group.

These animals will cheerfully take on opponents many times their own size, will never take a backward step, and will fight to death when cornered. They are also some of the most efficient predators imaginable.

A weasel (which is not that much bigger than a gerbil) will catch and kill a rabbit much greater than its own size. An otter can be 60 times the weight of a weasel, so it's a good thing that they mainly feed on crustaceans, fish and molluscs, cos if they went after mammal prey, maybe we'd be about the right size for them!

Our Commn Otter filming experience began remarkably well. We were up in the west of Scotland to film with wildlife legend Terry Nutkins, who had kept 'tame' otters much of his life. He bears the evidence of his pets' attentions on his hands, which are missing two fingers completely and covered in huge scars from the day one of his pets was feeling a bit grumpy.

We were driving round the coast early one morning on the way to Terry's house when I thought I saw something diving at the shoreline. 'Stop!' I yelled and we pulled up at the roadside. The cameraman and I snuck down to the edge of the water, the offshore wind keeping our scent from the otter's sensitive nostrils, staying low so he wouldn't spot us. Ever so cautiously, we managed to get to within maybe 10 metres of the water.

Ssshhhh!

Then up he popped right behind me! We'd done our sneaking brilliantly well, and managed to get closer to a Common Otter than I had ever done before. As he played, I started to whisper to camera, and then out of nowhere the theme tune to a 1970s television series came blasting out of the cameraman's pocket. The otter disappeared instantly. The cameraman had forgotten to turn his phone off. As the area we were in was so remote there was very poor mobile phone reception but for some reason a freak spot of coverage cropped up right there on the bank, and the booming music was his phone. The otter didn't come back, and he still hasn't forgiven himself. Budding naturalists beware – if you're desperate to see an animal in the wild, don't forget to TURN YOUR PHONE OFF!!!

Over the next few days we had many sightings of otters along the coast, but never close enough to get decent shots. Despite being quite a large mammal, otters can disappear into seaweed like slithering Houdinis, ducking into holts (otter homes) or scrapes amongst the rocks. One minute these skilful hunters are clearly there in front of you, the next minute they have gone and you may not ever see them again.

Below Those long sensitive whiskers help otters find prey in murky waters.

Raft Spider
Dolomedes plantarius

Spiders are one of the most exciting groups of animals on the planet. There are spiders that twirl weapons of silk to catch flying insects, spiders that cast nets and spiders that spit sticky threads over their prey. One of my favourite types is found scuttling right across the surface of ponds. These are the Fishing or Raft Spiders, and one of the most impressive is found in the fens of eastern England.

These big, beautiful spiders with bright yellow go-faster stripes sit at the water's edge with their front legs touching the surface so they can sense the vibrations of prey running across the water. But they don't just catch prey from the surface; they're fully capable of diving and snatching up tadpoles and even small fish such as Sticklebacks.

First, catch your spider

It would have been nearly impossible for us to see the Raft Spider hunting in the wild, so our first aim was to catch one. We wandered out into the fens (flat boggy land with lots of rushes and sedges and pools of water) in search of our first spider. Wearing chest-high waders, we lunged out into the brown water.

The telltale sign we were looking for was the silken tent which serves as a nursery for the Raft Spider's progeny. The mother weaves this silken crèche and then lays a couple of hundred eggs within it inside a protective ball. When the spiderlings hatch out they can scuttle about the nursery tent in safety.

We found a big female sitting at the edge of an old nursery, even though her babies were long gone. She was a little old, and looked like she could do with feeding up – which we were about to help her out with. We put her in a fish tank, tailored as much as possible to resemble her natural environment, filled with reeds, fen water and all of the tiny invertebrates that make their home there.

Fangs for everything

I was a bit sceptical about how long we'd have to wait to see her hunting – after all, most animals take a long time to adjust when taken out of their natural environment. Well, this one took about five minutes. Our spider ducked down on a plant stem and hung beneath the water, tiny bubbles of air clinging to minute hairs on her body and legs making her look as though she was wrapped up in silver foil. She was really exquisitely beautiful, like a perfect robot spider.

Within seconds, a hapless Water Boatman had brushed by the legs of the spider, and she pounced, sinking her fangs deep into the insect and injecting lethal venom. The Water Boatman never stood a chance.

Our spider brought her meal back to the surface to finish it off, injecting more venom to break down the prey into a liquid meat milkshake. Watching in extreme close up as the spider tore into her meal of minibeast munchies was as spectacular as seeing a Crocodile tearing up a Wildebeest. There was no doubt that this Raft Spider was worthy of her place on the Deadly 60.

Left Bubbles of air create a robot!
Below A classic spider hunting pose.

Raft Spider

SIZE:
☠ ☠

SPEED:
☠ ☠ ☠

WEAPONS:
☠ ☠ ☠

DEADLY RATING:
☠ ☠ ☠

Peregrine

Falco peregrinus

Whenever people complain about British wildlife, saying it's all a bit tame and dull, and asking, 'Where are the Lions and Great White Sharks?', I smile, and bring to their attention the Peregrine. This astounding bird is really quite common in the UK – in certain places where I go rock climbing such as the Wye Valley or Cheddar Gorge you're almost guaranteed to see one, or at the very least hear their insistent flight calls echoing around the rocky places they call home. However common, the Peregrine is a very special bird indeed.

SIZE:
✕✕✕

SPEED:
✕✕✕✕✕✕

WEAPONS:
✕✕✕✕✕

DEADLY RATING:
✕✕✕✕✕

This British native is the fastest creature that has ever lived. EVER. There are many statistics bandied around about the Peregrine, but the most reliable suggest it can reach in excess of 180 miles per hour for short periods of time. Compare that with the Cheetah's 60-odd miles per hour, and the Cheetah becomes no more impressive than an ageing tortoise with a hip replacement. And bunions.

The thrill of the kill

These bursts of extraordinary pace are not just to show off to other birds of prey. It's all about how the Peregrines hunt.

They catch other birds whilst they are in flight, flying up above them then folding in their wings, taking on an aerodynamic dart shape and speeding downwards over short distances in a killing flight known as a 'stoop'.

To cope with the extraordinary forces imposed on the body at such speeds, the Peregrine has baffles in its nostrils which prevent the extreme air pressure squeezing its brain and causing the bird to black out.

Their pointed wingtips and narrow tail form a characteristic anchor shape in flight which greatly reduces drag, and their ability to use every environmental feature to their advantage is extraordinary, as we were to find out.

The Peregrine will even fly upwards towards the sun when in pursuit of its quarry, so the bird it's hunting will have no idea where its killer is until it's all too late.

This is a devious trick that fighter pilots have been using since the time of the Second World War.

Top Gear test

To illustrate the Peregrine's sublime hunting skills, we hired an air force runway, a flashy convertible sports car, and Willow and Katy, two falconry birds trained to chase a lure for a reward of chunks of chicken.

We wanted to measure exactly what the Peregrine was capable of. Our idea was that I would drive the car down the runway while the birds' owner stood in the passenger seat waving the lure. The results were extraordinary.

As we accelerated, we'd pull away easily from the Peregrine as she took off. However, with no more than a few rapid wingbeats, the bird would be doing 50 miles an hour, and keeping pace with us as if she wasn't even trying.

Then, as she decided to make a move, she would soar up to about 10 metres above us – and she really did fly into the sun so we couldn't see her – before plummeting down at the lure.

It was then that the Peregrine really blew us away. She operated in a totally different world of speed to us.

The sports car, pedal to the metal, could do 0–60 in about 6 seconds. She did it in about 0.4 seconds! She hit the lure at 180 miles per hour and before we even knew what was going on, there was a flapping fury of razor sharp talons and tearing beak, right there in the car with us. We screeched to a halt, hearts racing, amazed at what we'd seen, and certain that this was one bird that deserved a place in the Deadly 60!

Above The fastest bird on the planet is also one of the most beautiful.

Goshawk
Accipiter gentilis

The basic difference between a hawk and a falcon is clearly shown when you put a Goshawk and Peregrine side by side. Their coloration is quite similar, though the Goshawk has a piercing bright orange eye and the Peregrine is much darker. However, the wings of the falcon are swept back and pointed, whereas the hawk's are more rounded with the flight feathers spread and finger like. The Peregrine's tail is rectangular and thin; the Goshawk has a magnificent broad tail shaped like a fan.

All these adaptations mean the Peregrine is built for flat out speed in the open skies, while the Goshawk is the master of manoeuvrability. They breed and hunt in dense woodland, swooping silently in and out of the trees until they finally nail their helpless prey. That can be anything from a vole or rabbit to another bird.

Bird's eye view
Amongst his collection of falconry birds, lovely Lloyd the birdman has a Goshawk, Ellie, a glorious seven-year-old bird who hunts just like a wild bird would. To fully understand how the Goshawk plies her trade in the dense woods, we had some serious technology to help us out. Ellie was fitted with a snug harness, and a miniature camera weighing no more than a triple A battery.

The images were beamed back via a satellite dish and recorded by one of our cameras, so for a few seconds at least, we could see how it would feel to be a pixie flying on the back of a Goshawk!

In order to get Ellie into hunting mode, I ran off into the forest carrying a lure on a falconer's glove. The thick leather glove was essential, as – with no warning whatsoever – she'd soar from behind a tree and smash into the lure at 40 miles an hour.

It was like being hit by a goose-sized jet fighter as she let loose enthusiastically with her razor-sharp talons and a tearing beak.

Bright-eyed killer
When we watched the video footage back we really began to appreciate the wonder of this miraculous bird. Most of the time she would effortlessly bank and weave among the trees in total silence, but every once in a while she would take a shortcut right between a fork in a tree – perhaps no more than a foot wide. Her wingspan was well over double that, and she would fold her wings beneath her in order to scythe through the gap.

She didn't break a single wingbeat doing it – she'd just

Goshawk

SIZE:
✖✖✖

SPEED:
✖✖✖✖

WEAPONS:
✖✖✖✖

DEADLY RATING:
✖✖✖

time her flight so perfectly that the folded downbeat happened at exactly the right moment. The sight was so beautiful we all caught our breath with the wonder of it.

I've only seen Goshawks a few times in the wild, and never hunting, but I live in hope because to see a Goshawk taking a rabbit must be one of the most dramatic sights in the world. This bird wonder is certainly worthy of inclusion on the list!

Right The exact moment our Goshawk folded her wings to zip through a gap in the trees. She didn't even break her wingbeats!

Adder

Vipera berus

Most people in the UK live their whole lives without ever seeing a reptile in the wild, and are certainly surprised to hear we have six of them. However, I know a few places where you stand a really good chance of seeing all six in a single day, and for Deadly 60 I was determined to do just that. We journeyed down to the Dorset Heaths, the best place in Britain for seeing reptiles, particularly on a warm spring day or in the middle of summer.

We were filming in late autumn, just about the time all those snakes and lizards are thinking about hibernation, and at that time of year seeing a reptlie is a pretty big ask. However, it all started perfectly. We had a divine hot autumn day, and a heathland reserve littered with slabs of corrugated iron – all placed deliberately to provide basking places for native reptiles. Beneath almost every slab was a Smooth Snake (Britain's third snake species, found only in the extreme south of England) and a few Slow Worms (a golden brown legless lizard).

Evil eyes on the prize

We managed to catch Sand and Common Lizards aplenty in amongst the heather, and got a Grass Snake at the end of the day. The Adder was the real prize though. I saw a good-sized male basking in the heather at the side of a path and leaped forward to catch him by the tail. He tried to make a break for it, so I gently supported his body with a twig, and lifted him up to show the camera. The first thing you

can't miss about the Adder is the evil-looking red eye. Then the thin neck, and typical arrow-shaped viper's head. Along its back the Adder wears a striking diamond shaped pattern – usually black in the males and brown in the larger females. Being vipers, the Adder's venom is haemotoxic, which means it poisons the blood, as I found out myself several years ago...

Having been all around the world catching venomous snakes, it's one of the most bizarre ironies of my life that the only one to bite me and put me in hospital was a humble Adder close to home.

Yup, an Adder, a poor unfortunate Adder who was lying minding his own business when I was out walking the dog and stepped right on him. He bit me right on the ankle, and for the next three days I was laid up in hospital in quite severe pain, and – I admit it – excruciating embarrassment. Particularly when the TV cameras turned up to film me in my moment of woe.

Even so, Adders remain one of my favourite British animals.

Adder

SIZE: ✕✕✕

SPEED: ✕✕✕✕✕

WEAPONS: ✕✕✕

DEADLY RATING: ✕✕✕

It does my heart good to know that there remains something wild and a little bit dangerous left in our safe British landscape. Something that can give a fully grown man like me a run for my money and puts on one of the most beautiful courtship dances of any animal into the bargain. But that's not the reason to put the Adder on the list. It's the fact that this viper can strike faster than a speeding arrow and take down its prey with a single bite that makes it Britain's top Deadly 60 contender.

Left Two male Adders (the darker snakes on the right) vie for the attention of one plump female.

Polar Bear

Ursus maritimus

It's not as easy as you might think to work out which animal is the world's largest carnivore. Grizzly Bears are generally much smaller than Polar Bears, but individuals in one population on the island of Kodiak in Alaska are unusually large, and some of them may be bigger and heavier than Polar Bears. However, if you're asking which is the more dangerous, there is no contest.

Grizzly) Bears are omnivores, and will eat totally different kinds of food depending on the time of year and where they're living; Polar Bears are full-on meat eaters. Their diet consists of warm-blooded mammal prey, like seal, walrus and whale. They live in freezing environments where food is in short supply, so if you encounter a Polar Bear out on the Arctic Ice, you will probably be seen as lunch.

Having a whale of a time

We'd travelled to Kaktovic in the Arctic north of Alaska, because it is one of the few places in the world where you stand a good chance of getting close to a Polar Bear. Kaktovic has become a hotspot for Polar Bear spotting because of the

The Polar Bear is one of the only animals in the world that would purposefully hunt and eat a human being. Their threat to humans is mostly down to their diet and chosen habitat. The three bear species of North America enjoy a sort of gradient of danger that directly relates to diet: Black Bears are mostly vegetarians, and are little danger to humans unless they feel threatened or are protecting cubs; Brown (or

locals' quota for hunting whales. Every year the Inupiat Eskimos are allowed to hunt three of the vast Bowhead Whales that feed along these coasts. These beasts can top 60 tonnes – equivalent to about half a jumbo jet, and once the community has used all the meat and blubber the bones are dragged to the shoreline. These skeletons form what appears to be a dinosaur graveyard, and the marrow and scraps are what draw in the bears.

At certain times of year, as many as 75 bears have been spotted scrapping and munching amongst the grisly remains. When we pulled up there were none to be seen, but we weren't expecting it to be easy. The seas had begun to freeze, giving the bears a chance to move out onto the pack ice in search of their seal prey, and whilst these solitary animals may endure the company of others, they certainly seem to prefer to go it alone.

Something in the air

Undeterred, we hired snowmobiles and roared out to the edge of the frozen sea to look out over the pack ice. There, sniffing the air was our first Polar Bear. It was the first I had ever seen, and was looked utterly wondrous shuffling about on the ice. He was perhaps 200 metres away, yet as soon as we stepped down to the shore, we clearly saw him lift his head and sniff the air; he had caught wind of us. If it had been a little later in the season when food is harder to come by, he would probably have made a beeline for us. Thankfully, he was obviously satisfied with the easy scraps at the bone pile, and he began to amble slowly off into the distance.

Then, two more appeared – a mother and her yearling cub perhaps a mile away in the distance. We watched through binoculars with growing excitement, until the cold was just so severe that we had to get back on the snowmobiles and head for Kaktovic before frostbite claimed our fingers and toes.

Even though they were at a distance, it was an unbelievable privilege to share the ice with this master of the frozen seas. The magnificent Polar Bear is a cert for the Deadly 60.

Left This guy looks like he'd love a big cuddle, but this is one furry beast you would NOT want to get close to.

Polar Bear

SIZE:

SPEED:

WEAPONS:

DEADLY RATING:

Wolverine

Gulo gulo

While we were waiting for our bear to show at the bone pile in Kaktovic, we got a rare and extraordinary surprise. A dark shape that started as a tiny dot in the distance, and slowly got larger and larger in our binoculars until it was discernable: 'Wolverine!'

The Wolverine is pound for pound one of the fiercest creatures on the planet. A super-sized weasel known for chasing bears from their prey and bringing down animals as large as moose – despite being no bigger than a Labrador wearing a shaggy yak's coat. He seemed to be making a beeline for the bone pile, and we could barely contain our excitement. Maybe 100 metres out, though, he got wind of us. All of a sudden he stood up on his hind legs, sniffing the air. He scuttled to one side and then to the other, standing up on his rear legs like a meerkat. An Arctic Fox was tagging along by his heels, not seeming to care much about the Wolverine's ferocious reputation.

Seldom seen

One of the guys who was with us had lived in the area for nine years, and had never seen a Wolverine before. Another had been there for 25 years and had seen one only twice, and at a distance. This was about to become a stupendous moment for all of us.

Sadly, he didn't come any closer, finally getting spooked and loping off across the frozen lagoon and into the distance towards a far off island. Minutes later, as we watched him disappear, three skidoos came racing out from Kaktovic in hot pursuit.

It quite warmed my heart to think that people who lived out here could have an interest

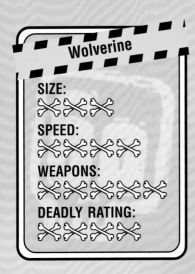

Wolverine

SIZE:
XXX

SPEED:
XXXX

WEAPONS:
XXXXX

DEADLY RATING:
XXXX

showing off the new ruff trimming her winter coat. It was made from fresh Wolverine fur.

A different view

Our great sadness at the loss of this rare and astounding beast had to be tempered with understanding for the Inupiat people who call this hostile place home. Their attitude towards wildlife is so different from our own. The animals there are a source of food and clothing, and have been for generations. Understandably, they don't take kindly to outsiders coming in and telling

in the rare wildlife that inhabited their world. Sadly this turned out to be romanticising the situation. The next day one of the Inupiat Eskimos came into our hotel

them what to do.

My own particular sadness though was only intensified days later down in the south of Alaska, when we spent a day playing with Jasper, a Wolverine that had been raised in captivity. He danced around in the snow, snapping at my heels, displaying fierce canine teeth in a jaw that is equal in power to a good-sized crocodile, and enables the Wolverine to chomp through frozen bone. His big hairy paws acted like snow shoes, helping him dance over the surface of the soft snow – the very mechanism that would allow him to chase down and kill animals as large as moose. Even in this almost tame animal, the tremendous guts, tenacity and personality of the Wolverine were clearly obvious. He was so wonderful that it made me mourn the slaughter of his wild compatriot all the more.

Far left Leaping for my lower legs with claws out and teeth bared – exactly the way he would attack prey as large as a moose… I was very glad that Jasper is semi-tame!
Left For guts and attitude the Wolverine has no competition.

Bald Eagle

Haliaeetus leucophalus

Earlier, I included the African Fish Eagle in the Deadly 60, and Bald Eagles appear to be very similar. So my idea was to go see the Bald Eagle gatherings in the snowy rivers of southern Alaska, but not to actually put the eagles on the list. However, what we saw when we got there really left us no choice.

Bald Eagle

SIZE:
✕✕✕

SPEED:
✕✕✕✕

WEAPONS:
✕✕✕✕✕

DEADLY RATING:
✕✕✕✕

First some statistics. The Bald Eagle can have a wingspan of around two metres, perhaps more in the bigger female birds. They fly in level flight at 30 miles per hour, but can 'stoop' (close their wings and drop out of the sky) at over 100 miles per hour, their huge curved talons puncturing right through their prey and causing massive internal damage and usually almost instant death. The thought of being a small animal minding your own business and having one of these monsters crashing out of the sky right at you is truly terrifying.

Something's fishy

The Bald Eagle's main food source is fish, snatched from the water on the wing. In autumn in southern Alaska, they feed on the glut of fish created as salmon head upstream to spawn, returning to the place they were born in order to lay their eggs.

Elsewhere in the world it is always a rare and exciting experience to see eagles, because a bird of prey of this size needs an enormous area to feed itself. Here, however, there is so much food that these birds congregate in their hundreds.

In order to try and get close to these huge clusters of birds, we decided to take an inflatable raft and float down river. It was a freezing day, with dense snow falling all around us, and the river water freezing to slurry despite being slightly warmed by geothermal activity. We certainly didn't want to fall overboard!

From the moment we were in the water the eagles were everywhere, thick in the trees like black crows.

The mature birds – over five years old – were wearing the extremely handsome classic white head and tail and black plumage, while the younger birds were more of a motley jumble of browns and black.

Who needs to hunt?

Along the shoreline crowds of eagles jostled for food, driving other eagles from salmon carcasses rather than bother with hunting for their own. The white riversides were littered with giant salmon as long as my arm, lying butchered in bloodstained snow amongst huge-clawed eagle footprints.

It was one of the great wildlife spectacles, all the more remarkable for me as a Brit – at any one time, I could look around me and count several hundred Bald Eagles, more eagles than we have living in the whole of the UK! Every one was a magnificent regal wonder, its talons capable of puncturing the skull of a sheep, its beak able to rip apart flesh and muscle. As they were so focused on their food, they allowed us to get to within just a few metres – way closer than I had ever been to a wild eagle.

Below The largest bird of prey in Alaska is the symbol of America. When a Bald Eagle's talons punch into prey they are as powerful as a Hyena's jaws!

Brown Bear

Ursus arctos

The Brown Bears are a group of animals found not just in North America, but through Europe and much of Asia too. Many groups of these bears have different common names, but grizzly is quite usual in America – grizzled refers to the golden brown mantle that these bears may develop when they reach maturity (other mammals such as sea otters become grizzled also).

Brown Bear

SIZE:
✕✕✕✕✕

SPEED:
✕✕✕✕✕

WEAPONS:
✕✕✕✕✕

DEADLY RATING:
✕✕✕✕✕

As I mentioned in the Polar Bear section, the Brown Bears found on the Alaskan island of Kodiak are probably the largest carnivores in the world, and it is the nightmare of every hiker to come face to face with one while out walking the trails. At certain times, the Grizzly is more dangerous than at other times. When they come out of hibernation in the spring they are lean and hungry. When they have cubs they may feel threatened and defensive. And watch out if they're surprised by a person walking up on them when they don't expect it.

Not to be sniffed at

So in wild American forests, suggested etiquette is to walk round loudly saying 'hey bear' every few minutes, so bears can hear you coming and make a sharp exit.

If the wind is in the right direction though, they may smell you coming from over a mile away. The nasal passages of a bear's skull are immense and filled with complicated flanges which expand the area of the sensing surface so much that they are considered to be seven times more efficient at sniffing than a bloodhound. And bloodhounds are a hundred thousand times more efficient than we are!

I've had some astounding Grizzly Bear encounters over the years, but the one we had filming Deadly 60 was remarkable because it was just so unlikely, and so close.

We had only an afternoon to go looking for a wild bear around the lake shores of southern Alaska, but as soon as I wandered down to the shoreline, I saw we had an advantage – perfect bear footprints running by the water, and very fresh indeed.

Without a moment to lose, we hopped into an inflatable boat, and headed off onto the glassy waters.

All around us, peaks that had never been climbed stood dusted with fresh frosty snow, dense pine forests covering their lower slopes. Surely we couldn't find a bear in this short period of time in all this wilderness? We skimmed to the other side of the lake, cursing ourselves for not having taken the time to put more clothing on. At the other side of the lake, Jonny the cameraman whispered urgently, 'What's that, Steve?' He was pointing to a tiny blob in the water ahead. I grabbed my binoculars...

Bear-ly there

It was a bear! We cut the engines and began to paddle closer, keeping our eyes glued to the bear as it headed up into the forest with a fish in its mouth. Despite her size, she disappeared from view the second she broke the treeline, her dark colours merging perfectly with the forest. We paddled closer and closer, and then suddenly she emerged again, just metres in front of us. Paying us no heed, she wandered along the shoreline for a good fifteen minutes, every once in a while dunking her head into the water and emerging with a huge salmon in her jaws, which she'd strip to shreds in a matter of minutes.

It was a real balancing act, making sure I didn't paddle us too close, as she could have leapt out into the water and been on us in just a couple of huge bounds. Grizzly Bears are surprisingly athletic – they can run as fast as a racehorse, climb pretty well, and swim superbly. We had to watch ourselves. However, she was much more interested in the salmon than in us, and she never gave us any sign of attack. There's no doubt though, that this magnificent beast, symbol of the wilderness, has to be on the Deadly 60.

Above The sight no adventurer wants to see, a Grizzly Bear in a bad mood!

Tiger Rattlesnake
Crotalus tigris

The Sonoran desert is like a film set for a Western movie, with huge Saguaro cactus silhouetted against a huge sky and Coyotes howling at a desert moon so clear it seems you could reach out and grab it. And if the desert itself is a movie, then the soundtrack is the tin-tacks-in-a-tobacco-tin sound of the rattlesnake.

This pit viper's rattle is formed from crusty domes of keratin (the material our fingernails are made from), extended every time the snake sheds its skin. The muscles that shake the tail are the fastest moving of any vertebrate, and the domes of the rattle vibrate against each other to make a noise that in a small rattler sounds like the buzz of a beetle's wings, and in the monster rattlers is a sound so deeply frightening that it will send any inquisitive animal packing in a millisecond.

Snoozing snakes

I had high hopes of heading out to look for rattlers in the wild, but we were in the Sonoran desert in the autumn, when many of the local reptiles were already hibernating, and others were at least feeling lazy. So after a bit of unsuccessful searching, we decided to hook up with a biologist studying rattlesnakes.

Matt Goode is a herpetologist (snake scientist) who has put radio tags into several hundred Tiger Rattlesnakes. The tag is implanted beneath the skin, and emits a constant radio signal. If you're tuned in to their frequency, you can track the snakes pretty accurately using a radio receiver, which makes it possible to find out endless amounts of information about the snakes' movements.

Matt has actually tracked a King Cobra moving over five miles in a day, which is revolutionary information. For us though, this technique was merely a great way of finding a snake. Even with the receiver it took us all day to find a tagged snake, as most of them were buried deep within piles of rocks. I finally pulled the first snake out from under a rock late in the afternoon.

The Tiger Rattler is quite a small species, but it's not to be trifled with. It's not even one metre long, with quite a small head and small venom glands, but the venom itself is extremely potent, and could certainly kill an adult human. However, it's their ability to kill small mammals that gets them on the Deadly 60.

Hot stuff

I mentioned earlier that rattlers are pit vipers. I remember as a kid thinking that this must mean they live in snake pits, which is a great idea, but not true! In fact, these snakes have an inbuilt super sense, a pit between the eyes and nostrils which senses the heat from the moving muscles of their prey. They can actually see heat, just as if they have a built-in thermal imaging camera!

The rattler will generally sit next to a game trail for hours, even days, biding his time until some unlucky mammal scampers past. Then, in the blink of an eye he strikes, gushes venom into his prey, and retreats. Within a matter of minutes the prey will be dead,

and the snake will follow the scent trail to his meal. With this hunting method, there is no danger of the snake itself being harmed. Rattlers may break this rule when they attack birds, in which case they'll strike, inject venom, and then hang on to the bird – otherwise the bird could fly off and succumb too far away for the snake to find it.

An intelligent, super-sensory serpent with fierce and fiery venom. This critter is definitely destined to be on the Deadly 60.

Tiger Rattlesnake

SIZE:
❌❌

SPEED:
❌❌❌

WEAPONS:
❌❌❌❌

DEADLY RATING:
❌❌❌❌

Below The blue and white stripes on this Tiger Rattlesnake were painted on his rattle so scientists could identify him.

Harris's Hawk

Parabuteo unicinctus

There are quite a few birds of prey on the Deadly 60, but this one made it for an unusual reason. Hawks generally keep their distance from each other, needing large territories to feed from. Harris's Hawks, however, are well known for enjoying each other's company. Even more remarkably, they hunt cooperatively with their mates.

Our first taste of this was out in the Sonoran desert with a Great Horned Owl we were trying to fly. The owl is a sworn enemy of this hawk, and if it encounters one by night, it will do its best to kill it. By day, however, the hawks have the upper hand, and within seconds of our owl being out in the open and calling, three wild Harris's Hawks had flown to within a stone's throw of us to take a look. I have no doubt that if we hadn't been there, the owl would have been torn to shreds.

Share and care

Whilst the hawks' social bonds can help them protect each other, it is when hunting that their friendships help them out most. A band of avian outlaws moves together jumping between dead trees, cactuses and fence posts, scouring the undergrowth with their extraordinary eyesight.

When one spots a mark, it dives into the bush, flushing the prey into the open, where his comrades swoop in to deal the death blow. Scientists believe that this method of hunting provides twice as much food for each bird as they would get if they hunted as individuals.

To get a closer glimpse of the hawks at work, we decided to film three trained falconry birds attacking a lure in the

manner they might use when hunting in the wild. I hid a small piece of meat with a long string attached to it inside a thicket, and bid a hasty retreat. The bushy camouflage was completely pointless, after all, this bird has eyes like...well, like a hawk!

With frightening speed, the first bird pounced into the bush, wings flaring to stop its furious-paced descent. As it hit the lure, I pulled the string violently, sending the lure skipping towards me like a frightened ground squirrel. Instantly, the other two birds swooped in and smashed into the lure, in an explosion

of dust and feathers. The bird who'd managed to snatch up the meat squatted over the food with its wings spread in a classic attempt to hide the prey from the others – apparently not be quite as keen to share the spoils as it was keen to share the hard work!

Harris's Hawk

SIZE:
✕✕✕

SPEED:
✕✕✕✕✕

WEAPONS:
✕✕✕✕✕

DEADLY RATING:
✕✕✕✕✕

Far left Harris's Hawks will make the most of any vantage point. Even Nick's boom pole!
Left The hawks' large eyes are said to be eight times more powerful than a human's.

Mountain Lion

Puma concolor

Of all the animals we looked for, the Mountain Lion could be the one we were least likely to actually find. People live their whole lives in Arizona (where we concentrated our efforts) without even seeing a sign of one, and we only had three days to try and get up close.

Mountain Lion

SIZE:
XXX

SPEED:
XXXXX

WEAPONS:
XXX

DEADLY RATING:
XXXXX

The Mountain Lion (also known as the Puma, Cougar or Panther) has a remarkable range, from the most southern countries of South America right up into Canada and Alaska. Nowhere is it particularly numerous, though, and it brings new meaning to the word 'elusive'. It's the second biggest cat in the New World after the Jaguar, and only slightly smaller than the African Leopard; a powerful and intimidating adversary should we actually succeed in getting close to one.

Caught on camera

Our first attempt to find the cat started with a biologist who'd placed remote camera traps in the mountainous deserts of southern Arizona. We trekked through several miles of dried-up riverbeds, stopping to examine the tracks and dung left by resident lions. The camera trap had taken photos of every animal that passed in front of it, and showed us glimpses of Skunk, Ring-tailed Cat, Black Bear, Deer, and then finally, two Mountain Lions who'd got right into the camera lens; one a male, then a few days later a female. It was a great sign. Even better was a call from another group of local biologists, who'd collared a Mountain Lion some months before to get information about its movements.

The satellite and radio collar was supposed to fall off automatically, but had failed to do so, so the group would have to try and catch the cat. They headed off into the mountains with hounds trained to track the scent of the lion barking excitedly with the thrill of the chase, and us following close behind. For the first few hours of the morning, we plodded doggedly through some of the most unfriendly desert I have ever experienced.

The Sonoran desert has more rainfall than most deserts, and thus much more plant life. However, it seems that everything there is designed to scratch, sting or impale the unwary hiker –

some of the cactuses had barbed hooks on the end of vicious spines as long as my thumb. If you so much as brushed them, they'd break off deep in your skin, and were excruciatingly painful.

Caving in

It was hot, harsh and frustrating – particularly as we didn't really think we'd see a lion at the end of it. But then all of a sudden, the hounds started to bay, the radios crackled into life, and all hell broke loose. The hounds had flushed out the lion, and it was coming down a steep-sided gully towards us. Shouts came through the radio:

'I see it! ... It's coming right at you! ... He's here, he's here!'

We raced down the gully to try and head it off, and arrived to see the vet fire a tranquillising dart and bring down the animal we thought we'd never find. Further down the gully, we found the dogs baying beneath a vertical rockface with a small cave at the top. 'We need a rock climber here, Steve,' called the chief tracker. 'He's in the cave.'

Having broken my back, leg and ankle in a climbing accident just a few months before, I was a bit nervous about climbing up to the cave, especially when I could come

face to face with a mountain lion at the top. However, the guys were on hand with their tranquiliser guns, so I dropped my bag and clambered up, dripping sweat, heart thumping fit to burst out of my chest.

When I got to the cave, I found a clear exit leading to the rock ridge above. The lion had scrambled up the vertical rock and escaped. We had lost him!

It was disappointing, but the lion's ability to give us the slip gave us ample reason to put this sublime survivor on the list!

Below A fearsome and beautiful predator, the elusive Mountain Lion stalks rocky rugged habitats.

Alligator Gar

Atractosteus spatula

The swamps of Louisiana are well known for one particular predator, the Alligator. However, we already had some crocodilians on the list and I decided instead to look for its namesake, the Alligator Gar — a predatory fish of prodigious appetite and proportions.

It was an animal I didn't know much about, and so when we arrived in the swamps, and I heard all the stories about two-metre long fish weighing twice as much as I do, I was pretty sceptical. But then I saw an Alligator Gar's skull. If you hadn't been told what it belonged to, you would probably believe it to be an actual Alligator skull — as long as my arm, broad and flat with bone heavier than any other fish skull I've ever seen, and sharply pointed teeth as long as my fingers. All of a sudden I was a little nervous about catching one of these monsters alive...

Our best bet for getting a gar was to set traps in the evening, and come back to check them the following day. They were simple traps, just a hook on a thick line tied to a big soft drinks bottle painted bright orange and then slung into the bayou (the wetland channels that run through the swamp). We could barely sleep that night for excitement at what we might find on our hooks.

The next day we stood at the bow of the boat scrutinizing the waters and reeds for the makeshift buoys. We'd thrown out 60 of the traps, but the first one we approached slowly started swimming away from us! Then, like a scene from *Jaws*, the drink bottle float was dragged below the surface of the water by

Alligator Gar

SIZE:
XXXXX

SPEED:
XXXXX

WEAPONS:
XXXXXX

DEADLY RATING:
XXXXX

clear out of the boat it was so strong. He fought bravely, but I managed to get him alongside and haul him onboard. It was an Alligator Gar; maybe 1.5 metres long, and heavy enough that it was a strain to lift him.

The gar is a real primitive fish, which has been around for tens, possibly hundreds of millions of years. They come to the surface to breathe air, have armour-like scales made of bone, and really do look like a dinosaur fish, more reptile than anything else. The tail, though, is much like that of the pike, fan shaped, and able to drive the gar in bursts of high speed.

They'll hunt anything: other fish, crabs, shrimp, wading birds, rats and other water mammals, even squirrels! We knew that once the hook was removed he'd be okay up on the boat, as gar have been recorded surviving out of water for several hours. We kept him just long enough to see his incredible teeth, then we set him free. We were elated at the result – and also elated to be intact!

something unseen which raced away with us in hot pursuit.

When I finally managed to grab the line and start to try and pull it in, the fish on the other end nearly dragged me

Left and below Believe it or not this Alligator Gar is a total minnow. These fish can grow to be half as long again, and twice as heavy as me!

Cottonmouth

Agkistrodon piscivorus

The swamps of Louisiana seem to have an awful lot of animals determined to make you uncomfortable, and keep you looking over your shoulder. Wading through the muddy waters with clouds of mosquitoes who actually seem to like the taste of antibug spray, you have no idea if you're going to step on a hungry 'gator or a venomous snake, of which the Cottonmouth is the most common, and the one people are most afraid of.

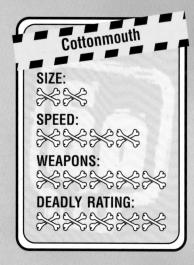

Cottonmouth

SIZE:
✖✖✖

SPEED:
✖✖✖✖✖

WEAPONS:
✖✖✖✖✖

DEADLY RATING:
✖✖✖✖✖

We were searching on a cool, rainy autumn day, the water was chilly round my knees, and as the afternoon wore on it seemed to be a terrible time to go searching for cold-blooded reptilians. Then Nick the soundman yelled out, 'Quick Steve, snake!!' I dashed back and just managed to grab it before it disappeared into the depths of the swamp, and it instantly showed me why it deserves its name, gaping open its mouth, and showing me the pure white, cotton-like interior.

Hiding the truth

Locals tell stories about Cottonmouths hiding in fields of cotton with their mouths open, camouflaged so they can bite people. This is nonsense. The Cottonmouth is actually not that aggressive, and certainly has no interest in biting a human he could never eat. As I gently restrained the cryptically coloured serpent amongst the leaf litter, he obviously just wanted to escape, but after a few seconds he curled up in a classic viper's coil, flickering the end of his tail in the leaf litter to create a sound like a rattlesnake's rattle.

The Cottonmouth is a small to medium sized pit viper that only rarely exceeds one metre in length, with a stout body narrowing to a thin neck, a large, arrow-shaped head with an evil, slit-pupilled eye and heat sensitive pits. There the similarity to other vipers ends.

The Cottonmouth is the most aquatic of all vipers, living the majority of its life in the water. Its scientific name 'piscivorus' means fish eater, and though these snakes will eat anything from bird chicks to small mammals, a good deal of their diet is of the swimming variety. While most pit vipers will strike and release their prey, when the Cottonmouth is hunting fish this is not an option (the fish could swim too far away after being struck before dying), so they strike the fish and hang on to it.

Just leave 'em alone!

As with all snakes, the threat they pose to humans is grossly exaggerated. According to the statistics, most snakes in the US actually only bite young men between the ages of 18–35 who've had too much to drink! Obviously, what this actually shows is that most bites occur when drunk guys trying to show off grab hold of a snake and get themselves in trouble. The Cottonmouth is no different. Sure, they'll strike if harassed, and have venom capable of killing a person, but actually they just want to avoid us. It's their ability to disappear into the background like a slithering phantom, to scare off animals as large as bear with their white gaping mouth, and to kill a fish in seconds that's earned them a place on the Deadly 60.

Below The gaping white mouth that gives this fabulous viper its name.

Alligator Snapping Turtle

Macroclemys temminckii

Somewhere in the dark, dank vegetation of the swamp lurks a cold-blooded killer. It looks like a dinosaur with the head of a dragon of your worst nightmares. Its beak has a cutting edge as sharp as a kitchen knife, and of all the Deadly 60 animals that vie for the title of 'beastliest bite', this one's most likely to win.

To find this creature — the Alligator Snapping Turtle — we went to the Black Bayou reserve in Louisiana with a team of biologists who've been studying these remarkable beasts for over a decade.

We journeyed out into the swamps armed with big hoop nets baited with chunks of fresh fish. Then we left the nets in some of the dankest corners of the bayou hoping that they would attract turtles.

The Black Bayou is about the most beautiful swamp in the world. Skeletons of Swamp Cypress trees draped with Spanish Moss reflect perfectly in the black water, which gives everything a kind of ancient fairytale feel. It was autumn ('fall' to the locals), and the

Alligator Snapping Turtle

SIZE:

SPEED:

WEAPONS:

DEADLY RATING:

trees were turning gold and crimson. If it wasn't for the massive mosquitoes biting clear through our clothes it would have been paradise.

Even so, the wonder of the place was tempered by disappointment when we came back the next morning to check our traps and found... not a thing.

Caught in a trap

The traps were totally empty. We spent most of the morning trawling through the swamps and every single net came up with nothing more than a few confused fish.

Then, just as we were giving up hope, I let out a little squeal of excitement. The final trap was definitely weighted down in the water. As I watched, a gargantuan head popped to the surface and took a gulp of air. And then another. And then another.

As we pulled the net over the side of the boat, Mitch, the biologist who was with me, let out a whoop of delight: 'There's three of them man! We've never had three in a trap before – and those two are HUGE!'

One turtle had a shell the size of my torso and was snapping furiously at the air. The other two were at least double the size. Mitch is a big guy, but the two of us had to strain every sinew to get the net into the boat, trying to avoid those lethal cutting jaws. These big guys were the heaviest Mitch's team had ever caught. It seemed that the Deadly 60 luck had well and truly struck.

Worm out of this one

I could only just lift the biggest turtle – it weighed almost as much as I do! I grasped the front of the carapace, desperately avoiding the turtle's extendable neck. The head alone was about the size of a volleyball, most of it muscle that drives the powerful jaw.

On its tongue was a wriggling piece of pink flesh that looked like a worm. Fish are attracted to this lure and when they get close to investigate they swim right into a death trap. At one point I put a stick in close to the mouth to try and lift the lure to

show it to the camera. The snapper's maw clapped shut like a steel trap and the stick was history.

Not everyone agrees which animals should make the Deadly 60 and sometimes you might think, 'Steve's just wrong on this one.' There's no way that's going to happen with the alligator snapper!

Left After almost giving up hope, we were rewarded with one of the biggest beasts the biologists had ever seen.
Above The turtles' dark colouring helps them hide from unwary prey.

Caribbean Reef Shark

Carcharhinus perezi

Sharks are the most refined, elegant, highly developed predators on the planet. The Deadly 60 crew just can't get enough of them. Yet many people believe that sharks are killing machines that will go into a feeding frenzy at the first scent of blood and begin thrashing around biting at anything and everything that gets in their way. This is nonsense.

Caribbean Reef Shark

SIZE:
✗✗✗

SPEED:
✗✗✗✗✗

WEAPONS:
✗✗✗✗

DEADLY RATING:
✗✗✗✗

In fact, in 2007, *one* person was killed by sharks *worldwide*. Just one. In the same year, millions of sharks (as many as 70 or even 100 million) were killed by people, mostly by having their fins hacked off for shark fin soup before being thrown back into the sea to die.

And what about the fabled 'feeding frenzy', where sharks are said to go mad at the scent of blood, slashing at anything that moves? Well, the only way I could show what a feeding frenzy is really like was to create one, and get right in with the sharks.

You looking at me, chum?

Bimini in the Bahamas is home to Sharklab, the world centre for shark research. Just offshore is a rocky outcrop with a healthy population of sharks, mostly Caribbean Reef Sharks.

We moored in the lee of the rocks, and started 'chumming' the waters – pouring fish blood into the sea. Within minutes, the water was full of sharks; sleek grey thrashing reefies about two metres long were coming up to the surface and drenching everyone on the

boat as they swished their tails. When the sharks were at their most excited and numerous I took a deep breath and slid over the side of the boat into the churning waters.

It was instantly obvious that the sharks were far from blind to what they were attacking, and it wasn't me. Bait was being thrown right in front of me, and the sharks would swim right up and snatch it, then turn and swim off into the distance. At one point, two reefies collided right in front of me, and the larger of the two span off straight into my face, then thrashed out over the top of my arm. The guys in the boat were convinced he had taken my arm off, but he just left me a little shaken up, my heart

beating a wee bit harder ...
The sharks knew I wasn't food,
and they were paying me no
heed. The camera, though, was
a different story.

Smile for the camera!

I was using an underwater film
camera to get shots of the
sharks, and they were
fascinated by it, swimming
right into the lens. All sharks
have jelly-filled pores in their
snouts that are phenomenally
sensitive to electrical fields.
They use them to sense the
tiny electrical pulses all
animals create as their muscles
flex, honing in on the signal
from metres away.

This ability helps sharks
hunt for animals in the dark or
in murky water and it also
enables them to catch prey
hiding in the sandy seabed.

It was clear that these
sharks were picking up the
electrical fields created by
my running camera, and were
coming in really close to check
it out. However, the Caribbean
Reef Shark makes the Deadly
60 not for this supersense
but for its outstanding
flexibility. When it senses
vibrations in the water from
the movement of prey it can
just about fold itself in two to
get at its dinner.

With a sideways snap of the
jaws any poor fish swimming
alongside is a goner – and a
place on the list is assured!

105

Below This Caribbean Reef Shark
came pretty close, but I knew he was
after our bait, not out to get me.

Tiger Shark

Galeocerdo cuvier

Of all the shark species feared by humans, and most often implicated in attacks, Tiger Sharks are second only to the Great White. They have massive thick bodies and broad heads, and serrated teeth that can take chunks out of a turtle shell and even chomp through metal. The tiger is a leviathan among sharks, a very scary creature indeed.

Its reputation as a man-eater is overrated but the scavenging Tiger Shark isn't fussy when it comes to dinner. It's even been called a 'rubbish bin with fins' because it will eat anything, including garbage!

We had a unique chance to work with the folks at Sharklab to catch and release a Tiger Shark as part of their research. To do this, we put down a long-line: a rope as long as three football fields, with baited hooks running down its length.

After 10 minutes of hauling and finding nothing, suddenly there was a flash of pale colour beneath us – a Tiger Shark!

Everything went crazy as we heaved it up to the surface. The shark was thrashing around threatening to yank us into the sea, churning the water white with fury.

Please release me

We slipped a rope over his tail, I grabbed his dorsal fin and we held him close to the boat while I put a tag in and the guys measured him. After only a few minutes, he was

Left Those can-opener style teeth enable the Tiger Shark to make a meal out of anything.
Right Simon gets up close and personal with a Tiger Shark.

ready to release and I had the privilege of swimming off with him.

I dropped into the water, took hold of his dorsal fin and swam down into the depths, helping to move the water over his gills and giving him back a taste for freedom.

Unfortunately, his first instinct was to swim straight at Simon the cameraman, gape open his terrible mouth, and actually chew on the front of the camera! Simon's one of the most experienced underwater filmmakers in the world but I swear even he backpedalled with more than a little haste.

As we congratulated each other for a job well done, the camera boat got ready to return to shore. I had started hauling in the rest of the line when all of a sudden I saw something that made me yell out.

Novel gnashers
Coming up to the surface was the largest Tiger Shark I've ever seen. He hadn't actually swallowed any bait but was trapped by a loop of rope curled round his tail. We pulled him

alongside us in flabbergasted awe; he was a monster!

As he relaxed, I gently opened his mouth to show the camera his teeth. Amazingly, sharks also have teeth-like scales over their whole body. They are called dermal denticles and, like sharks' regular teeth, they fall out and are replaced continuously.

If you stroke shark skin in one direction it feels as smooth as silk but if you stroke it in the other direction it will rip the flesh off your hands. The dermal denticles help protect the shark's body from damage and they also help sharks to swim super-efficiently by changing the way water flows around their body.

This fantastic feature has been mimicked in swimsuits of Olympic swimmers.

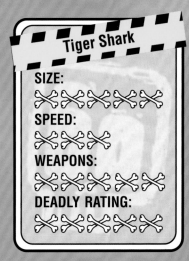

Tiger Shark

SIZE:
✕✕✕✕✕✕

SPEED:
✕✕✕

WEAPONS:
✕✕✕✕✕

DEADLY RATING:
✕✕✕✕✕✕

When the researchers had finished their work I hopped back into the water and took hold of his immense dorsal fin. Slowly he started to swim and with a helping push his powerful tail flukes drove him on and he disappeared into the big blue. It was one of the most majestic sights I have ever seen.

Great Hammerhead Shark
Sphyrna mokarran

Over the years I've been lucky enough to share the water with almost every notable species of shark but I had never encountered one that I've been fascinated by since I was a young boy: the Great Hammerhead. I've come across Scalloped Hammerheads many times – they often school in their hundreds around seamounts and are quite a common sight for the diver – but the Great Hammerhead is another thing altogether.

Great Hammerhead Shark

SIZE:
XXXXXXX

SPEED:
XXXX

WEAPONS:
XXXXXX

DEADLY RATING:
XXXXX

These solitary giants can be over six metres long (as big as all but the greatest of Great Whites) and live for up to 50 years. They are active predators, hunting down rays and other sharks, and also using their amazing electro-sensory system to detect crabs, lobsters and bony fish.

Nowhere to hide

All sharks have receptors in their snouts that can sense the tiny electrical pulses given off by the moving muscles of their prey – and if the prey isn't moving even its beating heart will give it away. The receptors are spread out along the Great Hammerhead's broad head, which scientist believe makes this shark even more efficient at homing in on dinner. Studies have shown they are sensitive enough to pick up the charge of a buried AA battery from 10 metres away.

One day after we'd been filming Lemon Sharks, Simon the cameraman had a hunch just as the sun began to go down, and wanted to get in the water. It seemed insane; we couldn't see any sharks around the boat for the first time all day, and when it starts to get dark sharks actually do start to hunt and get aggressive.

However, I believe that when someone has a hunch, you just have to go with it, so Simon and I jumped in and headed down for the bottom.

Shark and awe

As I sank down, expecting a long, bored wait for nothing, I saw a huge shape in the blue behind Simon. It was a shark with a giant sickle-shaped dorsal fin at least a metre high and a vast tail sweeping side to side with inestimable power.

Simon was filming with his back to the shark, and the shot shows me pointing in disbelief,

then frantically jabbing my finger at him yelling, 'I don't believe it, Great Hammerhead, Great Hammerhead!'

As he turned around – probably thinking that I was just pulling his leg – the shark swam straight for him, sweeping his hammer-shaped head along the sand, seeking out hidden prey with his electric supersense as we watched in amazement .

He swam right up to the camera, shook his head no more than a hand's breadth away and then slowly turned and headed off to circle us.

This impressive creature could certainly have made mincemeat of us, although records show only two confirmed human kills by Great Hammerheads throughout history. We didn't feel any fear, just the certainty that we'd had

an encounter with one of the most special creatures in the ocean; one that must surely be a contender for the Deadly 60.

Above Scientists have lots of ideas about why the Great Hammerhead's head is such a strange shape. The most popular theory is that it helps them hunt for prey at the sea floor.

Lemon Shark
Negaprion brevirostris

Lemon Sharks have been implicated in just 10 unprovoked attacks since records began in the 1500s and no one has ever been killed by one. On our perfectly planned trip, though, we only narrowly avoided being bitten, due the stupidity of other divers!

Amazingly, these sharks can change colour in just a few days if their environment changes. When they're hunting over sand their underbelly stays the classic lemony colour, but if they end up hunting over a muddier surface they start turning brown.

Our first meeting with Lemon Sharks was among the mangroves of Bimini in the Bahamas, where the tangled roots provide a perfect place for young fish to hide. Here we found young Lemon Shark pups that looked like bananas as long as my arm. Once we'd caught them we rolled them over onto their backs to put them into a state known as 'tonic immobility', which means lying motionless, almost in a trance.

Stomach turning stuff
While they were in this condition we studied what they had been eating by 'everting' their stomachs – literally pulling the stomach inside-out through the shark's throat. Many species of sharks actually evert their stomachs regularly to get rid of inedible food or other material.

Our encounter with adult Lemon Sharks was way out to sea on a shallow sandbar. We began to 'chum' the water, pouring fish blood and chunks of old fish into the sea, and within a few hours our first lemons had arrived. We were in the water with them as soon as we could get our tanks on.

The sharks were certainly curious, but they moved slowly and cautiously around us, not showing any sign of attacking. After a couple of days like this

Lemon Shark

SIZE:
✕✕✕✕✕

SPEED:
✕✕✕✕✕

WEAPONS:
✕✕✕✕✕✕

DEADLY RATING:
✕✕✕✕✕✕

we probably became a little complacent. That's inevitably when things go wrong.

Watch out... for humans!

Without telling anyone, the scientist we were with brought a bag of dead fish in order to hand-feed the sharks. Then without warning he handed the bag to director James. A little bit spilled out and one of the sharks turned its head and tore the bag apart.

Blood and dead fish went everywhere and suddenly about 15 Lemon Sharks were zipping about snapping up the fish! At least it was a great demonstration of their ability to work out that we weren't food, as none of us got bitten.

The second incident wasn't our fault at all. The captain of another boat swam over to us, clearly wanting to show off for the camera. He freedived down and grabbed a shark by its tail trying to ride it – not very smart, as lemons are some of the most flexible sharks in the sea and can easily snap round and bite something right next to their tail. When the shark tried to swim away he wouldn't let it go and it thrashed around, clearly stressed, until it got loose from him.

Then it made a beeline for Simon the cameraman and actually sank its teeth into the light on top of the camera. If

Simon hadn't reacted quickly he could have lost an arm. It was a reminder that if you push top-of-the-line predators too far things will go wrong.

That close call could be recorded as an attack, for which sharks will inevitably suffer. For me, it confirmed that the Lemon Shark should definitely make the Deadly 60 for its flexibility, its camouflage colouring and its obvious intelligence!

111

Left This young Lemon Shark pup was about to be utterly entranced!
Below Lemon Sharks often lie quietly on the sea floor. Scientists think they may be waiting for small fish to come and clean them of parasites.

Black Piranha
Serrasalmus rhombeus

The American president Theodore Roosevelt was the first person to put about the story that the piranha is a death-dealing frenzy fish. After a hunting expedition in Brazil in 1913 he wrote about seeing a cow fall into the river and having its flesh stripped to a bare skeleton in less than a minute.

Black Piranha

SIZE:
XX XX XX

SPEED:
XX XX XX XX

WEAPONS:
XX XX XX

DEADLY RATING:
XX XX

Yet I have spent days wandering around piranha-infested rivers and have never been bitten, and marathon swimmer Martin Strel swam the entire 3,000 mile length of the Amazon without an injury.

I have only ever witnessed the fabled feeding frenzy in dry times when water levels are very low, food is scarce and starving piranhas are forced to live in unusually high densities. At such times, you can hang a chunk of meat over the side of your boat and the water will churn and boil as fish scrabble to tear the food apart. Even then, it will take 10 or 15 minutes for them to demolish a pound of flesh. Mr Roosevelt's description was exaggerated, to say the least.

Safety catch

Although bites can be very serious when they do happen, healthy humans wading or swimming in a piranha's environment during normal high-water times of year are in little danger. This was brought home to me a few years ago in northern Amazonia.

We'd thrown a net across the mouth of a small river to try and find out what fish were living there. As we started to haul in the net it became trapped on a log and after a few minutes trying to free it I decided to dive into the murky waters. I dived down to the bottom and pulled the net up bit by bit, cutting it away from the log so that we could free it. We were in for a shock.

The net was FULL of Black Piranha, all of them about as big as the head of a tennis racket, their ferocious teeth snapping shut like steel traps! We stopped counting at 30.

One even got hold of the side of the boat, and with a terrible noise like fingernails being dragged down a blackboard its teeth scored deep gouges in the metal . However, for all their ferocity, not once did they try to attack me.

A tearing hurry

Black Piranha can be found hanging around rapids and in the deep parts of rivers. During the daytime they totally rule the river, ruthlessly shredding other fish, crabs, mammals, lizards and insects.

For much of the time they will focus on sneakily tearing chunks out of the fins and tails of other fish. Few fish are caught in the Amazon without scars from their encounters with Black Piranhas.

The piranha's teeth really are razor sharp and they're spaced out on the top and bottom jaw so that as the mouth closes they interlock. The jaw is so powerful that people who have been bitten on the finger or toe have lost the whole lot – bone and all!

In a feeding frenzy, a piranha will swim in, tear off a chunk of meat and swallow it whole, but whilst eating it will quickly swim away from the food source allowing another piranha in to take its mouthful. The cycle is like a conveyor belt of powerful little fish, and this is what makes the water boil and large prey

animals disappear down to the bone.

As with so many Deadly 60 animals, the Black Piranha is not quite the demon it is sometimes made out to be, but it certainly deserves to be on the list. It's the lord of the jungle deeps, and anything that

crosses its path at the wrong time is history!

Above Although the Black Piranha has a fearsome reputation, it's actually quite a timid creature most of the time. But when times get tough these fish certainly know how to bite! The powerful jaws and interlocking teeth can chomp right through bone.

Pink River Dolphin

Inia geoffrensis

The Pink River Dolphin, also known as the Boto, is one of the most extraordinary creatures in the world, odd in every aspect of its makeup and behaviour. The most striking thing, which is impossible to describe, is just how pink they can be!

It was an utterly surreal experience the first time I saw the lurid pink form of an adult river dolphin breaking the surface of the dark Amazon like a weird water worm with a bulging round head and a long, thin beak full of teeth.

Despite the name, not all Pink River Dolphins are pink; in fact, they can be bluish grey or even white. Unlike other dolphins, the bones in the neck are not fused, so these strange animals can turn their heads right around, look over their own shoulders and even catch fish swimming behind them.

Stunning stuff

These bizarre creatures share many of the features of marine dolphins, including an echolocating supersense which they use to find fish in the soupy murk of the rivers they live in. Scientists think they can use high-powered bursts of ultrasound to confuse or stun their prey, and, like all dolphins, they are extremely intelligent, conversing with each other in a series of clicks and whistles.

The only thing they seem to lack compared to other dolphins is good eyesight. However, spend any time in the Amazon and you'll see that this doesn't really matter – the water is so murky that visibility is usually absolutely zero.

It's likely that the other senses of the Pink River Dolphin are highly developed but as so little is known about these remarkable mammals, we can't yet be sure.

Friend or foe?

On some of my Amazonian expeditions, dolphins were an almost constant companion.

Pink River Dolphin

SIZE:
✖✖✖

SPEED:
✖✖✖✖✖

WEAPONS:
✖✖✖

DEADLY RATING:
✖✖✖✖✖

They seem to enjoy interacting with people, and will come right up to boats, sometimes even popping out of the water to get a better look at you.

Traditionally, fishermen would accept dolphins raiding their nets and taking some of their catch, as the animals were believed to be sacred reincarnations of people.

Nowadays, as the old ways are being lost, more and more people see the dolphins as a nuisance and they are even killed by angry fishermen.

Dam building, overfishing and pollution also threaten the future of river dolphins all around the world.

Tragically, most biologists believe the Yangtze or Chinese river dolphin became extinct in 2006.

Despite the threats from people, the Pink River Dolphin still sits firmly at the top of the food chain in the depths of the Amazon and Orinocco rivers and its intelligence, twisty-turny body and ultrasonic supersenses all place it solidly in the Deadly 60.

Above and left The outstandingly flexible Pink River Dolphin is super-effective at finding fish in the murky Amazon even though it has quite poor eyesight.

Goliath Bird-eating Spider
Theraphosa blondii

This extraordinary spider is an arachnophobe's nightmare, with a legspan as big as your head and fangs as long and sharp as cat's claws. The common name was chosen by an early Victorian explorer who claimed to have seen one eating a hummingbird, and there have been several accounts since of these colossal invertebrates feeding on birds.

Goliath Bird-eating Spider

SIZE:
✕✕

SPEED:
✕✕✕

WEAPONS:
✕✕✕✕

DEADLY RATING:
✕✕✕✕✕

However, it is the exception rather than the rule for these spiders to eat birds. They may take hatchling birds nesting on the ground, or perhaps finish off an injured bird that falls near to their burrow, but as these spiders are terrestrial, they would only very rarely come into contact with birds they could kill and consume.

Beware of the hair

Having kept lots of large tarantulas over the years, I've developed an enormous amount of respect for these extraordinary beasts. Each individual has its own personality, and most of them won't bite in defence, although they will kick hairs off their abdomen in response to a threat. These 'urticating' hairs float up into the air, and have tiny spines on them which sting, itch and irritate the skin of anything nearby. If they get into your eyes, throat or nose, the reaction can be quite serious.

The Goliath Bird-eating Spider will also rub its legs together to create a kind of hissing sound to repel attackers; a bite really is a last resort. The venom is said to be no more serious than a wasp sting, but judging by the length of the fangs, a bite would be much more painful, and would probably result in a nasty infection. However, they are generally totally harmless to people unless they are really pestered, and it's their hunting skills that put them on my list.

Mercurial marvels

In Amazonia, these spiders are so numerous that in a good location you can find 20 or 30 in one good searching session, and with a little practice coax them out of their holes. My first of the evening crouched in the entrance to her burrow with maybe 30 spiderlings clustered around and over her; they poured back into the hole like quicksilver when we walked by. Another spider bristled expectantly as I stroked a piece of grass over the hairs on her legs. I eventually took hold of one leg and pulled her gently out – not something I'd usually attempt with a tarantula as it would be a sure fire way to get a pair of giant fangs buried in your finger.

Her cephalothorax (the head and body not including the abdomen) was about the size of a tablespoon head, and her legs spilled out over the side of my hand. She soon calmed down so dramatically that I had her walking over my hands like a tame pet tarantula, and even managed to flip her to see her huge fangs. Surely even the most hardened arachnophobe would have warmed to this spider superstar!

However, they are far less genteel when it comes to feeding. The spiders will sit motionless, waiting to sense vibrations from potential prey nosing close to the mouth of the burrow. Then they lunge forward, almost too fast for the eye to register. The mouse, cricket, or yes, even the bird, will be injected with venom in the blink of an eye.

This sublime skill definitley puts this amazing arachnid on the Deadly 60.

Below Despite its name, the Goliath Bird-eating Spider only rarely feeds on birds. This chick was one of the unlucky ones!

117

Fer de Lance
Bothrops asper

The lancehead snakes are the most feared creatures in Central America, and for good reason. These venomous beasts, which can grow to a muscular 2.5 metres long, are responsible for more human deaths than any other American reptile. The name 'Fer de Lance' (French for 'spearhead') comes from the malevolent shape of the head. Even snake lovers have to admit this is one evil-looking serpent.

It's not the most venomous snake I've worked with, but the first Fer de Lance I ever caught, in Costa Rica, certainly provided my most frightening snake encounter. This snake very quickly showed me why the species has such a ferocious reputation and taught me a few etremely scary lessons.

As I got close to his curled body the snake struck at me repeatedly – and not in threat display, but really trying to bite me. That's something snakes only rarely do. Then, instead of trying to escape, he chased me! Many people believe that snakes will always chase you, but in fact they almost never

actually do. Everyone around scattered like screaming skittles! That was the only time in my career I have genuinely been chased by a snake.

What was most impressive, and quite unnerving, was how far the Fer de Lance struck.

I thought I knew how far vipers can strike from the coiled position, but I didn't realise that the Fer de Lance uses its unusually heavy body as an anchor, whipping its arrow-shaped head through the air like a missile. It launched almost its entire body length in strike! I now know you need to be almost two metres away to be safe.

With my heart pounding, I asked the cameraman to leave the camera on the ground rather than get up close to film.

Vicious vipers

As a snake lover, I don't usually like to dwell on their negative aspects; they have a bad enough reputation already, generally undeserved.

To me, snakes are the most beautiful and fascinating of creatures. They are hugely beneficial to the ecosystem as pest controllers and apex predators, and they are rarely even seen by people let alone a threat to us.

The Fer de Lance is an exception. This is mainly due to its dangerous habit of sitting motionless by game trails until a soon-to-be-lunch rodent passes by. Unfortunately, humans use those trails too and the Fer de Lance may well attack humans who tread too close, using its enormous fangs and lots of potent venom. Many people die or are disfigured by them every year.

The frightening fer

But it's not their threat to people that puts them on the list. It's their brain-boggling perfection as a predator.

A Fer de Lance can hang about motionless for days at a time waiting for its prey of small mammals or birds. Then, the second an unlucky creature comes too close... BAM! It whips out in the blink of an eye, and before the prey is any the wiser the venom has been delivered and the snake is ready to eat dinner.

It's also been reported that

this species is developing an ability to spray its venom much like the spitting cobras. This could eventually mean it doesn't need to bite attackers to fend them off. I think this aggressive snake would need to change its attitude completely before it changes its behaviour – I don't think it will stop biting any time soon!

Rivalling the King Cobra as the most frightening snake I've ever encountered, the Fer de Lance is a dead set cert for the Deadly 60.

Left The Fer de Lance usually feasts on rodents and birds, but sometimes other small vertebrates will do. This snake is eating an ameiva lizard.

Electric Eel
Electrophorus electricus

Over the years many animals have taken me by surprise, but none have given me as big a shock as the Electric Eel. These large, heavy-bodied fish, which have to come to the surface to breathe, are some of the ugliest, weirdest looking animals you'll ever see. They can grow to about 2.5 metres long, and weigh about 20 kg – as much as a large dog! And it gets weirder...

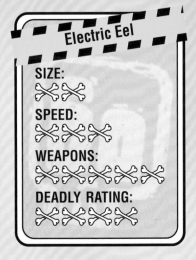

Electric Eel

SIZE:
✕✕✕

SPEED:
✕✕✕✕

WEAPONS:
✕✕✕✕✕✕

DEADLY RATING:
✕✕✕✕✕

Electric Eels have three pairs of organs in their abdomens that can produce an electric charge of up to 500 volts – plenty enough to kill an adult human at close range.

They live in the eddy pools beneath rapids in murky Amazonian waterways, where they use their ability to vary the power of their electric weapon to defend themselves and also to stun fish and small mammals. My encounter with an Electric Eel was a shock in more ways than one.

On a lengthy expedition filming in the Amazon rainforest some years ago, the base camp was at the bank of a large river which provided everything we needed – drinking water, fish to eat, a place to swim and bathe. Each day, it saved us from the swelter and claustrophobia of the forests.

Caiman look at this

One morning, we were greeted by a 3.5 metre Caiman basking at the riverside. This dangerous crocodilian was ominously watching our every move so I decided to catch him and move him on for the safety of the camp.

He was no more than five metres away from me but because he was taking shelter in an overhanging bush I couldn't get at him. So I tried to attract him to the beach.

After several hours watching me slap the night-time waters with a chunk of dead fish, the rest of my team began to lose interest and wandered back to bed, leaving me splashing around on my own at the water's edge. And then it happened...

It was as if someone had hit me with a baseball bat out of nowhere. I was thrown clear off my feet and landed flat on my backside several metres away from the river. All the hairs on my arms stood up .

I knew instantly what it was and staggered up to the camp yelling, 'Electric Eel, guys, Electric Eel!!' The camera crew all leapt out of bed in their pants, and ran down to the river with me, no doubt thinking I was making it up. They were to get a genuine surprise, and an encounter they would never forget.

Feeling around for food

The eel had come up out of the depths, and was actually half out of the water on the bank, squirming around rather grotesquely, trying to find the prey that it had stunned. It was awe-inspiring: dark brown on top, bright orange beneath and as thick as my calf muscle.

Once it realized there was no meal lying unconscious on the bank, it slid silently back into the murky water, but several times over the next hour it came back up to check out what was around.

Fish biologist Phil Wickens, who spent many years studying the Electric Eel, told me I had got off lightly. In fact, for me to have survived the attack with such a mild (!) shock, Phil estimated the eel could have been as much as four metres away under the water. Another lucky escape, and another denizen of the deep on the Deadly 60!

Below The Electric Eel's an unattractive beast, but it's still a stunner. Special organs can produce enough electricity to kill a human.

Golden Poison Dart Frog

Phyllobates terribilis

So just what is the most poisonous animal in the world? A snake? Nope. Perhaps a scorpion? Keep guessing… A spider? Stingray? Venomous fish? Not even close. In fact, the most toxic animal in the world – by quite a considerable distance – is a tiny jewelled frog which lives deep in the jungles of Colombia. The adult frog is at most about 5 cm long, about the size of my little finger!

Golden Poison Dart Frog

SIZE:
✕✕

SPEED:
✕✕

WEAPONS:
✕✕✕✕✕

DEADLY RATING:
✕✕✕✕✕

Columbia's beautiful Golden Poison Dart Frog is one of about 120 species of dart frog. Most are very brightly coloured, which is a sign to let potential predators know they are not good to eat, although the strength of the poison varies from species to species.

Some species have a mild poison, which just doesn't taste very good. In other species, the poison is so strong that it could kill an inquisitive dog that made the mistake of sniffing too close.

Scientists believe that all dart frogs gather poisons from insects they eat, and then secrete a much more potent version of the poison from glands on their skin.

The Golden Poison Dart Frog almost seems to have a chemical weapons factory inside its body, turning those poisons it eats into the most lethal animal toxin known.

It's said that just one tiny frog could contain enough poison to kill 10–20 men, 10,000 mice, or 2 elephants – although no one has actually done an experiment to prove this, of course!

Dangerous diet

Remarkably, if this frog is kept in captivity, it will lose all of its poison. This makes it almost certain that it is something in the frogs' diet that leads to the creation of the poison. It is likely to be Choresine beetles, which themselves get their poisons from chemicals in the plants they eat.

What I can tell you from personal experience is that even touching a less poisonous dart frog is hazardous, because the poison seeps through your pores and gets into your bloodstream.

I once examined frogs of a much less toxic species and after I had been holding them for a few minutes I nearly keeled over feeling as drunk as a skunk!

The fatal blow

The 'dart' part of the name comes from the hunting technique of the Chocó and Cofán people who share the forests with these miraculous little frogs.

They catch the frogs and rub arrows or blowpipe darts over their back to collect the poison. If that arrow or dart is then fired into a monkey, the unlucky beast will drop out of its tree stone dead within a matter of minutes.

Even though these frogs use their bright colours as a warning and they don't kill directly, I don't think anyone will argue with me if I put the most poisonous animal in the world on the list!

Below It's hard to believe that this gorgeous golden jewel of a frog can produce the most potent animal toxin in the world.

Army Ants

Ecitoninae

In Central and South America, native people live harmoniously enough with venomous snakes and scorpions, and they'll even endure the attentions of malarial mosquitoes and bathe alongside flesh-eating fish. The one thing they do not ever try to combat is the army ant.

In fact, if a trail of marauding army ants enters a village, all the people will move out, and they'll only come back once the ants have moved on. This may seem extreme in a world full of modern insect-repelling techniques but even today nothing can deter a raid of several million of these ferocious biting beasts. Instead, the locals have learnt to value these irregular visits.

Marching munchers

As the ants tear through a village they consume everything in their path, killing the cockroaches, centipedes and scorpions that live in the roof rafters, driving out snakes, rats and mice, and generally doing the greatest spring cleaning job known to man!

Locals have to be very careful to take with them everything they don't want to lose though, as army ants have been recorded overcoming and eating animals as large as goats and chickens.

Unlike many ants which form static colonies and build nests, army ants are nomadic, making temporary nests known as bivouacs as they travel. Remarkably, groups of ants form these nests out of their own bodies, forming walls by holding on to each other with their mandibles and legs. Inside, the queen and her eggs are kept safe by the ferocious soldiers, whose jaws can easily pierce human skin.

Tribal people even use army ants to close wounds – they make an ant bite each side of a gash then break the head off so it stays in place like a stitch!

Relief in the river

I have had many encounters with army ants, but the worst was on an expedition to Colombia many years ago.

I was fast asleep in my hammock when suddenly I was woken by horrendous pain. Army ants had come through our camp on a raid and they were all over me. Just minutes later, as I was leaping up and down pulling ants from every inch of my body, the others in the group started yelling too. It was utter chaos! The only solution was to go and sit in the river, shivering miserably and waiting for the dawn.

When I think about that experience I'm left in no doubt that for their ability to act together as a terrifying team, their total dominance of any animal no matter how large and their ability to sweep through the forest like a shifting shroud of death, army ants are definitely on the Deadly 60!

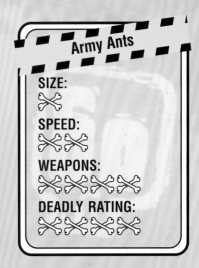

Army Ants

SIZE:
☠

SPEED:
☠☠

WEAPONS:
☠☠☠☠

DEADLY RATING:
☠☠☠☠

Left With long legs and a stretched out body, army ants look almost spider-like.
Below Helped by special hooks on their legs, these ants are forming a temporary nest called a bivouac.

Common Vampire Bat
Desmodus rotundus

This flapping mammal has an awful lot to answer for. Of the 1,100 different species of bats around the globe, the vast majority eat either fruit or insects. Three species found only in Central and South America do not, and their grisly reputation may be responsible for the fact that many people all over the world fear bats.

Each bat needs to consume about two tablespoonfuls of blood each day, which for an average-sized adult is about 60% of its bodyweight. Needing to eat this much food to survive is quite risky and if a bat were to fail to find food for a few nights it could starve.

That's just sick!

Female bats overcome this problem in an unusal way: by regurgitating blood for their friends and family. One bat will approach another and groom her for up to two minutes. The animal being groomed will then regurgitate part of her meal for the grooming bat to lap up. That's true friendship!

Those three species are all vampire bats. All the myths, legends and stories about vampires, blood-sucking bats and Dracula originate from them. Two species seem to prefer to prey on birds; only the Common Vampire Bat specializes on mammal blood.

Vampire bats are actually pretty tiny, with bodies about the size of a gerbil and a wingspan no greater than my forearm. However, the fierce canine teeth are some of the largest (relative to body size) in the animal kingdom. One bat that I caught in a mist net in the rainforest turned its head right around to bite my thumb, and pierced through my thick leather gloves and nearly down to the bone. The pain was excruciating, and I had a few worries about rabies as the bats spread this nasty disease.

Young bats are also fed in this way, which leads to a pretty stinky home. Walls of roosts (in caves, tunnels and hollow trees)

Common Vampire Bat

SIZE:
☠☠☠

SPEED:
☠☠☠

WEAPONS:
☠☠☠☠

DEADLY RATING:
☠☠☠

can be black with congealed blood and there's often a very strong smell of ammonia.

Urine trouble

The vampires fly close to the ground seeking a scent trail to lead them to a potential meal. When they're within range, they drop down, and scrabble and hop along with one of the most grotesque movements of any animal.

Special heat sensors in the nose guide them even closer and allow them to select a part of the animal that is full of hot blood. Once in position, they bite the skin and lap up the flowing blood, feeding for up to 20 minutes at a time.

Incredibly, the bat's spit contains chemicals that stop the blood clotting, and even an anaesthetic that prevents the animal feeling the pain of the bite. These chemicals are so effective that scientists are experimenting with using them in medicine.

Within a couple of minutes of starting to eat, the bats start to urinate, getting rid of useless plasma from their meal so they don't become too heavy to fly.

Pretty horrid, but as one of the most freaky and fascinating of all animals, and the owner of the world's most impressive set of gnashers, I just had to include them on the list.

Above The Common Vampire Bat is small, but I wouldn't call it cute!
Left Super-sharp teeth and a grooved tongue help bats to feed on blood.

Index